If It Ain't Woke, Don't Fix It

Ben Shapiro

Creators Publishing
Hermosa Beach, CA

If It Ain't Woke, Don't Fix It
Copyright © 2022 CREATORS PUBLISHING
All rights reserved. No part of this book may be reproduced or transmitted in any form or by any means, electronic or mechanical, including photocopying, recording or by any information storage and retrieval system, without permission in writing from the author.

Cover art by Muge Li

CREATORS PUBLISHING
737 3rd St
Hermosa Beach, CA 90254
310-337-7003

Although the author and publisher have made every effort to ensure that the information in this book was correct at press time, the author and publisher do not assume and hereby disclaim any liability to any party for any loss, damage or disruption caused by errors or omissions, whether such errors or omissions result from negligence, accident or any other cause.

ISBN (print): 978-1-949673-87-6
ISBN (ebook): 978-1-949673-88-3

First Edition
Printed in the United States of America
1 3 5 7 9 10 8 6 4 2

A Note From the Publisher

Our goal is to make you think. We want you to react. We want you to respond.

Since 1987, the writers we represent and publish start discussions, arguments and even controversies. Love them or hate them, you can't ignore them.

Beginning with print and evolving into digital, Creators has been at the forefront of the media industry. We have been disrupting the status quo since our company was founded on the premise that creators should own their work, characters and ideas. Decades later, we continue to evolve as society pushes forward and technology changes.

At Creators, we support creators.

—Creators Publishing

Contents

UnCultured — 1

The Lies Tearing America Apart	2
Get Ready for 4 Years of Media Sycophancy	4
The Inequality of 'Equity'	7
When the Hateful Think They Are the Virtuous	10
It's Time to Uncancel Americans	13
The Authoritarian Left Is on the March	16
When Lies Matter More Than Facts	19
Wokeifying America's Military	22
Why Dr. Seuss Had to Go	24
The Circular Logic of Systemic Racism	27
Due Process Is the Opposite of Social Justice	30
For the Left, Bigotry Is a Tool	32
Past Time to Fight Back	35
The Fight Over Identity	37
The Muddled Thinking of 'Antiracism'	40
The Movement Against Critical Race Theory Is Deeply Necessary	43
Yes, It's Ungrateful to Turn Your Back on the National Anthem	46
Stop Surrendering Education to the Radical Left	49
The Narrative Is the Priority	52
Reality Remains Undefeated	55
The Left's War With Biological Reality	57
Whoopi Goldberg Says the Holocaust Wasn't About Targeting Jews. Here's Why That Matters.	60
The Attack on Joe Rogan Is an Attack on Dissent	63
The War On Parents Continues	66

The Slap Heard Around the World	69
The Left Is the Culture War Aggressor	72
The Anarchic Philosophy Behind 'LGBTQI+ Pride Month'	75
Roe v. Wade Is History, but the Abortion Debate Reveals Rot at America's Center	78

Pan(dem)ic 81

How Bureaucracy Killed Hundreds of Thousands of Americans	82
Lying About 'Misinformation' To Justify Tyranny	85
When Does the COVID-19 Panic End?	88
Welcome to the Forever Pandemic	91
An 'Abundance of Caution' Mentality Leads to Tyranny	94
The Big Government COVID-19 Lie	97
The Year of Living Unreasonably	100
The COVID-19 Impact of Expressive Individualism	103
Canada Goes Tyrannical	106
The COVID-19 Authoritarians Panic over the End of the Mask Mandates	109

Newspeakonomics 112

How Blue City Governance Is Destroying Blue Cities	113
Our Empathetic Authoritarians	116
When Politicians Call For 'Fairness,' They're Usually Lying	119
No, Government Spending Isn't 'Zero Cost'	122
The Nation in the Bubble	125
The End of Risk and the End of Civilization	128
Punishing Achievement Is Punishing Everyone	131

The So-Called Meritocracy Isn't The Problem	134
The Death of California	137
The Great Re-Sorting Is Here	139
The Quest to Destroy Work	142
It's Time for the Market Pushback to Begin	145
Yes, It's Biden's Inflation	147
The Elitists Who Want to Rule the World	150
Joe Biden's Economy Is a Disaster	153

The World Stage — 156

This Is Not Normal	157
Biden Sets Everything on Fire	160
If You Side With Hamas, Your Anti-Semitism Is Showing	163
China Isn't Winning. The West Is Forfeiting	166
What Foreign Dissidents Understand About the American Flag	169
The Demise of the Love Gov	172
America's Slow Suicide	175
Our Elective Monarchy	178
The Red Wave, and the Democratic Suicide Strategy	181
Putin Wakes up the Western Ostrich	184
Environmentalist NIMBYism Means Foreign Policy Disaster	187
Push Where There's Mush	190
The Death of The Elite 'Center'	193
The Chinese Know We're in Cold War II. It's Time for Us to Understand the Same.	196
Buzzword Foreign Policy Makes for Failure	199
Salman Rushdie, Iran and Joe Biden	202
Unserious Leadership in A Serious Time	205
Forgetting 9/11	208

The International Anti-Woke Backlash 210

About the Author 214

UnCultured

The Lies Tearing America Apart

January 13, 2021

Last week, the Capitol was breached by a group of fringe Trump supporters who had bought into a series of lies: the lie that President Donald Trump lost the election due to proven voter fraud and irregularity; the lie that the Electoral College results, legally certified state by state, could be overturned by Congress or the vice president; the lie that Trump would remain in office if only some sort of armed rebellion were to prevent the election certification by Congress. Those were lies. And those lies had deadly consequences.

Thankfully, the vast majority of Americans don't believe those lies. Which means we should be able to unify around certain basic truths: that Joe Biden is legally president-elect of the United States; that violence in pursuit of political ends is a deep wrong and those who participate in it should be punished to the full extent of the law; that broad claims regarding invasion of rights ought to be backed by compelling evidence.

But we won't.

That's because while the Democratic Party and the political left agree that Joe Biden is president-elect, they absolutely disagree with both the fundamental precept that violence in pursuit of political ends is a deep wrong and the even more fundamental precept that claims require evidence. We saw that this summer when Democratic Party officials made light of riots spreading across the nation in the name of yet another lie—the lie that America is systemically racist, rooted in slavery and Jim Crow, and replete with bigoted police dedicated to endangering black lives. Democrats demanded no evidence to support those claims; in knee-jerk fashion, they simply repeated ad nauseam untruths about the existential threat to black Americans in the United States. Which means that for the Democrats and the political left, violence is fine so long as it supports their narrative, and un-evidenced claims are fine so long as they support an agenda.

In order to defend such violence, the political left has mobilized behind another convenient and advantageous lie: the lie that the Capitol riots represent all conservatives and Republicans. Paul Krugman of The New York Times suggested that the "putsch was decades in the making," chalking up the rioting to "Republican elites" since before Ronald Reagan. The Washington Post amplified a nutty post from the chairman of the Nye County Republican Party in Nevada into a referendum on a "long-festering struggle within the Republican Party over conspiracy theories, purity tests and fealty to the rule of law." Members of the media gleefully hunted for Republicans to blame for the Capitol riots, calling for the deplatforming of brand-name conservatives and cheering on social media crackdowns.

Lies are dangerous. And double standards are perhaps the most dangerous form of lying: They grant the bravery of purity to those most willing to defy decency, prompting similar spasms of cruelty and malice from the other side. The solution to our national crisis of conscience isn't bad-faith political purges or repetition of tiresome falsehoods about the nature of the United States. It's truth.

But truth is more a shield than a sword. And we are now in the age of swords, wielded aggressively by those with little principle but an unending sense of their own moral superiority.

Get Ready for 4 Years of Media Sycophancy

January 20, 2021

On Sunday, Jan. 17, Vice President-elect Kamala Harris sat down with Jane Pauley of CBS News "Sunday Morning." Pauley treated Harris to a full-on journalistic massage. At no point was Harris asked a tough question; at no point was Harris treated as anything other than an idol worthy of worship. Perhaps the most awkward manifestation of this sycophancy came when Harris—an extraordinarily and transparently manipulative and mechanical politician—spouted a canned speech about relentlessness. "I was raised to not hear no—let me be clear about it," said Harris. "I eat no for breakfast!"

This prompted a spasm of ecstasy from Pauley, who immediately reflected Harris' bizarrely inappropriate laughter with an enormous grin of her own.

It will be four long years.

For four years, the media complained that outgoing President Donald Trump treated them as an enemy. They self-servingly claimed that they were *actually* the protectors of democracy and individual rights. It took all of one month after Trump's inauguration for The Washington Post to add the slogan "Democracy Dies in Darkness" to its masthead. By October 2017, CNN began running ads explaining that it was all about "Facts First."

Trump, for his part, attacked the media whether they deserved it or not: Every disparaging headline, true or not, became "fake news." That was unjustified and wrong, obviously. But the media's lack of credibility wasn't solely attributable to Trump. It resulted from their own journalistic malfeasance for years on end during former President Barack Obama's administration—"his only scandal was wearing a tan suit!"—followed by their aggressive repetition of even the most thinly sourced scandal regarding Trump.

And now we'll return to the gaslighting of the Obama era, when members of the Obama team could openly *admit* to lying to the media, only to receive obsequious praise in return. Already, media outlets are praising the newfound veracity of Biden's press team—despite the fact that Jen Psaki, Biden's choice for White House press secretary, was accused of openly and explicitly lying to the media in 2016. Media members are even admitting that the vacation has begun: CNN's Jim Acosta—and, ladies, find you a man who loves you like Jim Acosta loves Jim Acosta—admitted that he'd be covering Biden differently, explaining, "If being at the White House is not an experience that might merit hazard pay... then perhaps it is going to be approached differently."

Of course, Acosta never needed hazard pay. He was too busy declaring himself a hero and preening for the cameras while pulling down a lucrative book contract. But now that the Biden administration is a reality, our media can go back to sleep.

And so, the controversies of the day will turn to the trite. The big question won't be governmental oversight but media self-policing: Last week, the media were consumed with the vital question of whether Vogue magazine's cover of Harris is respectful enough, given that it shows her wearing her trademark Converse sneakers. Other major controversies to come will include just how cute Joe Biden's dog is and whether the racial diversity of his Cabinet is merely important or *super* important. Meanwhile, the same media outlets that act as stenographers for the Democratic

Party will insist that other outlets meet with social media censorship. After all, American needs unity! And that unity can only be provided by the same people who have wrecked all pretense of institutional objectivity in the pursuit of partisan outcomes.

People will continue to seek information from alternative sources, of course. But that will only provoke the media to seek new methods of repressing those alternatives. As it turns out, the commitment of many in our media isn't to truth or facts. It's to monopolistic control.

The Inequality of 'Equity'

February 3, 2021

President Joe Biden took office pledging a return to unity and decency. A new era of good feelings is at hand, we were informed by both his administration and its sycophants in the media. A new world—a world of "equity"—is at hand.

Equity, you see, is the word of the day. Not *equality*—that would be a traditionally American concept. The Declaration of Independence declares that "all men are created equal... endowed by their Creator with certain unalienable rights." The 14th Amendment to the Constitution provides that all citizens must receive "equal protection of the laws." Equality, in the traditional understanding, means something simple and easy to implement: the protection of the rights of all individuals, along with the invasion of none of those rights.

Equity means something different. The two words are separated by one syllable—but that syllable represents the difference between justice and injustice, rights and infringements, individualism and tribalism. Equity, in the common political parlance, means that each *group* should receive the same outcome as every other group. Ibram X. Kendi, the chief expositor of the new Democratic "racial equity" theory, explains that "Racial equity is when two or more racial groups are standing on a relatively equal footing." Because race is a social construct, says Kendi, the chief indicator that two races are on unequal footing can be found *not* in proof of differential treatment by race but in differential *outcome* by race.

To prove racial inequity, therefore, one need not show animus or discriminatory policy. All one must show is unequal *outcome*. Kendi explains in his massive bestseller, "How to Be an Antiracist": "A racist policy is any measure that produces or sustains racial inequity between racial groups. An antiracist policy is any measure that produces or sustains racial equity between racial groups." And, says Kendi, "There is no such thing as a nonracist or race-neutral policy." *All* policies either forward equity or oppose it. Any policy not *explicitly designed* to rectify unequal outcome is therefore racist.

This philosophy is both idiotic and perverse. It's idiotic because all human groupings—literally all of them—will result in differential outcomes. Draw a line down the middle of any room in random fashion and the result will be unequal income distribution, criminal records, educational histories. When culture takes a hand, disparities can be more deeply rooted than random chance. Discrimination would still not be the cause of such disparity. As a basic logical matter, discrimination is not the cause of all disparity.

This philosophy is perverse because it attributes malice to those who have none; it fosters policy that *actively discriminates*, supposedly in order to alleviate unproven discrimination. Kendi himself explains: "The defining question is whether the discrimination is creating equity or inequity. If discrimination is creating equity, then it is antiracist. If discrimination is creating inequity, then it is racist."

Unfortunately, this idiotic and perverse philosophy has become the root of Biden administration policymaking. "Equity" has been used as the keyword from environmental to economic to COVID-19 policy. Susan Rice, Biden's domestic policy adviser, explained this week, "(W)e're focused on racial justice and equity...It's for everybody who has not had the benefits of a system that has not served everybody. ... This is not about serving one group to the detriment of another." This, of course, is a lie. It is utterly about group equality, which requires individual injustice.

America was rooted in equality and freedom. Equity requires freedom to be curbed. It's therefore a national tragedy to watch equality of rights abandoned in favor of equity. If freedom is discarded to achieve equality of outcome, we no longer live in an America defined by the Declaration of Independence. We live in an America defined by tribalism and leveling—and, in short order, tyranny.

When the Hateful Think They Are the Virtuous

February 10, 2021

This week, Virginia Heffernan, a columnist for the Los Angeles Times, unleashed the most perverse column in recent memory. The title: "What can you do about the Trumpites next door?" Heffernan wasn't lamenting neighbors who had tagged her house with pro-Trump graffiti, or who had participated in the Jan. 6 riots, or who had even held an election watch party and turned the music up too loud. No, Heffernan was lamenting the travails of living next door to Trump supporters... who had cleared her driveway of snow.

Heffernan writes, "Trumpites next door to our pandemic getaway... just plowed our driveway without being asked and did a great job." This simple act launched Heffernan into a journey of angst and rage. "How am I going to resist demands for unity in the face of this act of aggressive niceness?" she laments. "I realize I owe them thanks—and, man, it really looks like the guy back-dragged the driveway like a pro—but how much thanks?"

In order to justify the answer she wants to give—as little thanks as possible, because, after all, these are Evil Trumpites—Heffernan proceeds to speculate as to her neighbors' motives: Perhaps they only cleared her driveway because she and they were white. Or perhaps this whole event was a reminder that members of evil groups sometimes do good—she compares them to the Shiite terrorist group Hezbollah, Nation of Islam leader Louis Farrakhan and the Nazis. If she treats her neighbors with too much decency, she reminds herself, that might make her like an upper-middle-class family from France who collaborated with the Nazis and lamented the Nazis' defeat because of their commitment to being "polite."

Heffernan seethes with the agony of cognitive dissonance. "My neighbors supported a man who showed near-murderous contempt for the majority of Americans," she writes. "They kept him in business with their support. But the plowing."

In the end, Heffernan's solution is to be nice—but not *that* nice. She will offer a "wave and a thanks," but she is "not ready to knock on the door with a covered dish yet." She's unwilling to give her neighbors "absolution," ignoring the fact that they have not asked for absolution, nor do they require absolution for the great sin of voting differently and *clearing her driveway of snow*. "Free driveway work, as nice as it is," Heffernan states, "is just not the same currency as justice and truth." The only way she'll be able to truly treat her neighbors decently is if they recognize "the truth about the Trump administration" and work "for justice for all those whom the administration harmed." Then, she'll be decent to her neighbors.

Heffernan's neighbors should immediately pile as much snow as humanly possible back onto her driveway, hose it off and let it freeze.

The nasty snootiness Heffernan evidences is all too common these days. Heffernan obviously judges her neighbors not on the basis of what she knows about them but on stereotypes she holds about all Trump voters. When faced with the reality that those who disagree with her can be nice and decent people, she simply dismisses the possibility altogether, justifying her own viciousness by referencing their supposedly radical political beliefs. Which, of course, makes her the villainess in this particular morality play.

But she's too blind to see it. These days, tens of millions of Americans are. And so, the social fabric continues to shred, all in the name of depraved, unearned moral superiority.

It's Time to Uncancel Americans

February 17, 2021

This week, actress Gina Carano made headlines when Disney+ and Lucasfilm decided to cancel her from their hit series "The Mandalorian" over controversial social media posts. It is perfectly obvious that the corporations had been looking for an excuse to get rid of Carano thanks to her conservative politics—The Hollywood Reporter uncovered a source who snarked, "They have been looking for a reason to fire her for two months, and today was the final straw."

What, precisely, was Carano's sin? After the 2020 election, she put up a social media post decrying voter fraud and then put up a post referring disparagingly to elite-driven mask culture. This week, she put up a post pointing out that the Holocaust did not begin with mass murder but with neighbors turning on one another thanks to politics. The Holocaust comparison may have been overwrought, but it was certainly not anti-Semitic. "Nonetheless," Lucasfilm stated, "her social media posts denigrating people based on their cultural and religious identities are abhorrent and unacceptable."

Carano's cancellation came the same week as the cancellation of "The Bachelor" host Chris Harrison. Harrison's sin: He said that one of the contestants on this season of "The Bachelor" ought to be given "a little grace" over having attended a sorority party with an antebellum theme several years ago. Harrison said, "I have seen some stuff online—this judge, jury, executioner thing—where people are just tearing this girl's life apart and diving into, like, her parents, her parents' voting record. It's unbelievably alarming to watch this." And the woke authoritarians emerged to deem him racist.

Carano's and Harrison's responses, however, were polar opposites.

Harrison immediately kowtowed to the mob. He issued a mewling statement, no doubt at the behest of his corporate overlords, in which he suggested that he is now following a "path to anti-racism" and explaining, "My words were harmful. I am listening, and I truly apologize for my ignorance and any pain it caused you." Not a single person could have explained how asking for "a little grace" for a young woman who had sinned by wearing a Scarlett O'Hara-style dress had harmed anybody. But that didn't matter. The only one harmed was Harrison, whose apology was deemed insufficient. He has self-banished to the cornfield for at least this season, and maybe forever.

Carano, by contrast, took down the Holocaust post because she realized it was overwrought. But she didn't apologize. And, more importantly, she made a ballsy move: She signed a deal with my company, The Daily Wire, to produce and star in a new film. She explained: "I am sending out a direct message of hope to everyone living in fear of cancellation by the totalitarian mob. I have only just begun using my voice which is now freer than ever before, and I hope it inspires others to do the same. They can't cancel us if we don't let them."

We at The Daily Wire are dedicated to that simple proposition. It's time for the American people to stop allowing themselves to be canceled. The institutions of American culture are arrayed against individuals who think differently, from Hollywood to corporate America to the establishment media. But dissenters can band together, too, and support one another. Those who believe in open dialogue—people across the political aisle—need to come together. Otherwise, the authoritarians will continue their march toward woke dystopia.

The Authoritarian Left Is on the March

February 24, 2021

This week, Democratic Reps. Anna Eshoo, D-Calif., and Jerry McNerny, D-N.J., sent out a series of letters to America's largest communications corporations: AT&T, Alphabet Inc., Cox Communications, Dish Network, Comcast, Apple, Amazon and others. Their letters demanded answers from these corporations on one simple topic: Why would these platforms continue to allow the dissemination of "misinformation" from conservative outlets?

"Our country's public discourse is plagued by misinformation, disinformation, conspiracy theories, and lies," the House Democrats wrote. "These phenomena undergird the radicalization of seditious individuals who committed acts of insurrection on January 6th, and it contributes to a growing distrust of public health measures necessary to crush the pandemic. ... Are you planning to continue carrying Fox News, Newsmax, and OANN?"

The overt move by members of the government to cudgel private corporations into silencing unpopular viewpoints was clearly violative of First Amendment principles. The Constitution clearly provides that Congress shall make no law abridging freedom of speech or the press; Democrats have now hit upon a convenient workaround where they bully private actors into doing their censorious bidding.

This clever gambit is rooted in the conflation between "disinformation" and "misinformation" promulgated by the establishment media since 2016. After the 2016 election, the media went berserk with the theory that Hillary Clinton had lost the election thanks only to Russian interference. "Russian disinformation"—meaning false information promulgated by a foreign government for the purpose of interfering in domestic politics—had twisted the election. Now even disinformation promulgated on American soil is protected by the First Amendment. But it soon became clear that the authoritarian left wasn't interested merely in active disinformation springing from foreign sources. It was troubled by *any narrative or information that contradicted its point of view*. This information could quickly and easily be labeled "misinformation."

And "misinformation," it said, had to be policed.

Why, precisely, wouldn't the answer to misinformation be factual rebuttal? Because, the authoritarian left argued, misinformation led to "incitement." Now, there is a legal standard for "incitement"—and it's a high bar to reach. But the authoritarian left has broadened out the meaning of incitement to include any verbiage that elicits strong emotions... so long as conservatives are responsible for such verbiage. Thus, it's possible incitement to call people by their biological pronouns but perfectly innocent fun to wink and nod at widespread looting and rioting.

The answer to "misinformation" and "incitement," however, can't lie within government. So Democrats have turned toward hijacking the private instruments of informational dissemination, all in the name of reestablishing an informational monopoly the left lost with the death of the Fairness Doctrine in 1987, and with a monopoly that collapsed completely with the rise of the open internet.

And corporations are going along with all of this.

This week, Amazon banned a book on transgender people, "When Harry Became Sally," presumably because it took a non-woke line on the subject. Coca-Cola is now apparently indoctrinating its employees into the cult of Robin DiAngelo "anti-racism." Facebook and Twitter and Google are all preparing new measures aimed at cracking down on "misinformation"—opaque guidelines and nonrigorous standards that will surely cut in favor of the same establishment media now pushing censorship, and the Democrats they support.

    The establishment media are fond of saying that we're experiencing a crisis of authoritarianism in America; they point to the criminal acts of Jan. 6 and suggest that right-wing authoritarianism threatens democracy itself. The far greater threat to democracy, however, lies with an authoritarian left that is now ascendant in virtually every powerful institution in America.

When Lies Matter More Than Facts

March 3, 2021

This week, The New York Times ran a long piece re-reporting a supposed race scandal from Smith College. The scandal, originally reported in midsummer 2018, featured a black student, Oumou Kanoute, who claimed that she was racially profiled while eating in a dormitory lounge. She suggested in a Facebook post that she was confronted by a campus police officer, who might have been carrying a "lethal weapon," and a janitor, adding: "All I did was be Black. It's outrageous that some people question my being at Smith College, and my existence overall as a woman of color."

The janitor was placed on paid leave. The college president issued a campuswide statement explaining, "This painful incident reminds us of the ongoing legacy of racism and bias in which people of color are targeted while simply going about the business of their ordinary lives."

The incident was reported by establishment media outlets far and wide.

There was only one problem: It was a lie.

A full investigation by an outside law firm found no evidence of bias. Kanoute was eating in a closed dormitory, and the janitor was doing his job. The campus police officer had no weapon.

So, did The Times apologize for its original coverage? Of course not. It turned the story into an investigation of supposed structural biases based on race and class. In one of the more astonishing sentences ever written in a major newspaper, The Times reported, "The story highlights the tensions between a student's deeply felt sense of personal truth and facts that are at odds with it."

For those who speak English, this sentence translates thusly: The story highlights the tensions between lies and the truth. But for those who speak the wokeabulary, this sentence actually makes equivalence between lies told on behalf of a self-serving victim narrative and factual truth. The two must be balanced against each other, not one dismissed for its patent falsehood.

This is the society we now inhabit: a society in which a "deeply felt sense of personal truth" must be weighed against "the facts." And typically, our society dismisses "the facts." That's because it has been infused with the spirit of deconstructionism, which sees all facts as merely a manifestation of how our social structures "define" truth based on cultural context. "Facts" are merely a reflection of how your society sees truth. But there's no reason your society's definition of truth must be the only one. In fact, a more tolerant society would make room for the expressive self-definition of "your truth" and redefine truth along individual lines; an accepting, kind society would allow a "deeply felt sense of personal truth" to flourish by requiring others to accept it as *fact*.

What of those harmed by that "deeply felt sense of personal truth"? This is where structural arguments about power come in. We can choose which sense of personal truth ought to triumph with reference to societal structures: Those who are deemed more victimized ought to be given more credibility. Thus, Nikole Hannah-Jones, de facto editor of The New York Times, declared that the janitor put on leave might have been the truly privileged one in the story: After all, "What is the social class of the Black student that this entire piece centers on? What is the actual power dynamic at play here?"

This is how we arrive at the insanity of a transgender

agenda that calls for banning books that demonstrate the unmalleability of sex: A "deeply felt sense of personal truth" is at odds with the biological facts, and the biological facts must lose.

In the end, perhaps the deconstructionists were right; perhaps a society's emphasis on facts, data and actual truth reflects the values of that society. Such a society values the individual, since facts are accessible to individuals and aren't the select preserve of a priestly caste. Such a society allows the possibility of consensus by appeal to verifiable facts. If facts don't matter, there can be no common polis—or there can only be a polis as dictated by those in power. And perhaps that's precisely the point.

Wokeifying America's Military

March 17, 2021

This week, President Biden's military declared its first war... on Fox News host Tucker Carlson. Carlson had committed the great sin of pointing out the oddity of the fact that the Biden White House had been promoting brand-new uniforms for pregnant soldiers, rather than America's military efficiency in the face of a rising Chinese military threat. This prompted spasms of apoplexy from top brass in the military itself: Pentagon spokesperson John Kirby said that the Pentagon was filled with "revulsion" at Carlson's comments, adding, "We absolutely won't just take personnel advice from a talk show"; Army Sgt. Maj. Michael Grinston tweeted that women "will dominate ANY future battlefield we're called to fight on," calling Carlson's words "divisive"; Marine Corps Master Gunnery Sgt. Scott H. Stalker, the senior enlisted leader of the U.S. Space Command, said that Carlson's opinion was "based off of actually zero days of service in the armed forces."

Now, the military itself recognizes that pregnant women can't exactly staff front-line positions. At 20 weeks of pregnancy, pregnant soldiers in the Army are exempt from field duty, deployment, wearing individual body armor, standing at parade rest or attention for longer than 15 minutes, or participating in weapons training; upon diagnosis of pregnancy, all pregnant soldiers are exempt from regular physical fitness training.

And the military has reported in the past that mixed units underperform all-male combat units. In 2015, a yearlong Marine Corps report found that, according to NPR, "all-male units were faster, more lethal and able to evacuate casualties in less time."

But the content of Carlson's words was less important than the reaction to them, for it was unprecedented for top members of the military to unite in excoriating a civilian opinion journalist. Had it happened on former President Trump's watch, the media undoubtedly would have used it as an example of politics infusing traditionally apolitical institutions. Dark buzzwords like "authoritarian" and "fascist" would have been tossed around casually. Yet when the military was mobilized to attack Carlson, the media cheered instead.

We are watching in real time America's institutions being gutted on behalf of left-wing politics. Formerly apolitical institutions are being remolded top down to reflect the values of our New Ruling Class: those who speak the wokeabulary, who believe in the tyrannical and polarizing theories of Ibram X. Kendi and Kimberle Crenshaw, who see their roles as the social engineers of their fellow Americans. This is true in our universities; it's true in our colleges; it's true at our corporations; and now it's true in the American military. No wonder we're told that our military will somehow be stronger for tossing out gender-neutral physical fitness tests, or paying for transgender surgeries, or forcing soldiers to read the asinine musings of critical race theorists.

Our military is designed to deter and to defend, to kill people and break things. If diversity facilitates that mission, that's wonderful. But to supplant the military's chief mission with the woke protocols of the political left is to undermine that chief mission. The world is a dangerous, ugly, competitive place. If our masturbatory woke solipsism blinds us to that reality, the cost will be quite real—far more real than any supposed threat emanating from the musings of Tucker Carlson.

Why Dr. Seuss Had to Go

March 10, 2021

This week, Dr. Seuss Enterprises announced it would stop the sale and distribution of six classic volumes from the great children's author. Those volumes, said the company, violate its commitment to "messages of hope, inspiration, inclusion, and friendship." The books include portrayals of people "in ways that are hurtful and wrong."

Society has long held that activity that damages others ought to be curbed. John Stuart Mill posited the so-called harm principle—the belief that activity that harms someone ought to be condemned or even barred—in the mid-19th century. But Mill refused to conflate harm and offense: Being offended wasn't cause for sanction of another.

Broadly speaking, society agreed with this formulation. But in the past few years, this formulation has been completely turned on its head. Now offense is not only considered a harm; it is considered the *chief* harm in our society. Physical injury, after all, is merely physical. But mental or emotional injury—that threatens our very sense of identity. Because we find our identity in our own sense of self-creation, any societal denial of that sense threatens our identity. As Carl Trueman writes in "The Rise and Triumph of the Modern Self": "The era of psychological man therefore requires changes in the culture and its institutions, practice, and beliefs that affect everyone. They all need to adapt to reflect a therapeutic mentality that focuses on the psychological well-being of the individual."

When individual self-creation becomes the chief goal of a society, institutions must be torn down—institutions, after all, foster a set of rules that may not be conducive to individual self-creation. Informational flow must be dammed—after all, information may allow others to take a different, objectively based opinion about you than you take subjectively about yourself. Books must be burned—after all, books carry with them implicit messages that may threaten your sense of yourself.

Iconoclasm becomes the order of the day.

Our societal turn from actual, measurable harm toward subjective, psychological harm places us on the road to complete devastation of our culture and our rights. Now anyone who offends—or even has the potential to offend—can be, and indeed ought to be, fired. Now any book—no matter how old or how inoffensive—can be, and indeed ought to be, banned. Now any kernel of information—no matter how true—can be discarded.

This formulation puts all power in the hands of those who are most easily offended—or at least those who claim to be. *The offense itself is the weapon.* Legal torts require damages; societal torts merely require a claim of damages, without evidence. No one can explain just how a drawing in "If I Ran the Zoo" has contributed to actual racism; there are no recorded incidents of a single white supremacist citing "And to Think That I Saw It on Mulberry Street" as a formative source in his racist worldview. But any academic with a computer and a degree in postmodern nonsense can take those books off the shelves simply by claiming that offense is *possible*.

In the end, the only literature allowed will be the literature that adheres to the values of our postmodern world—a world in which we are not expected to conform to societal rules but society is expected to conform to our own acts of self-definition. That means your child reading "I Am Jazz" but never—never, Gaia forbid!—the Bible. It means goodbye to cultural icons, large and small—goodbye to all vestiges of the past, replete with their "bigoted" value systems.

It means that the purges have only just begun.

The Circular Logic of Systemic Racism

April 28, 2021

Last week, ex-police officer Derek Chauvin was convicted of second-degree murder, third-degree murder and second-degree manslaughter. The evidence on the murder charges was weak; the evidence on manslaughter was significantly stronger. Still, the jury took only 10 hours and zero questions to come to its conclusion: guilty on all counts.

In and of itself, the Chauvin case never should have been a national news story. After all, an average of three suspects are shot by police every day in the United States, and thousands of homicides that have nothing whatsoever to do with the police take place in the United States every year. Theoretically, national news stories should be indicative of profound national problems, not man-bites-dog statistical rarities.

But, of course, that was the entire point of elevating the George Floyd story to national attention: to declare it indicative of a deeper rot at the core of America. Thus, Chauvin was convicted not of his individual criminal activity but of a charge that was never even brought against him: the charge of racism. As Minnesota Attorney General Keith Ellison admitted, there was no evidence whatsoever that Chauvin was a racist, or that his killing of George Floyd was motivated by race. "We don't have any evidence that Derek Chauvin factored in George Floyd's race as he did what he did," Ellison ruefully told incredulous "60 Minutes" host Scott Pelley. And Pelley, speaking for the entire establishment media—a left-wing bubble thoroughly invested in the narrative of systemic American racism—responded, "The whole world sees this as a white officer killing a black man because he is black."

Pelley isn't wrong. In the end, evidence for systemic racism is utterly unnecessary. Systemic racism requires no evidence of intent, either individual or systemic. It requires only evidence of disparate outcome by race. Which is why Ellison explained that even though he couldn't charge Chauvin with a hate crime, he could charge the entire system with racism in the Chauvin case: "In order for us to stop and pay serious attention to this case and be outraged by it, it's not necessary that Derek Chauvin had a specific racial intent to harm George Floyd. ... (P)eople of color, Black people, end up with harsh treatment from law enforcement. And other folks doing the exact same thing just don't."

Now, statistically speaking, this is simply untrue. In late 2020, the Bureau of Justice Statistics released a report that found no statistically significant difference by race between criminal activity and arrest—in other words, you get arrested in America if you are reported to have committed a crime, no matter your race. Multiple studies, from Harvard's Roland Fryer to professor Peter Moskos of John Jay College of Criminal Justice at City University New York, show that police officers are less likely to kill black Americans than white Americans in similar circumstances.

But to ask for evidence of systemic racism beyond mere inequality of outcome is to be complicit in systemic racism, according to the circular logic of systemic racism. Any incident of white-cop-on-black-suspect violence must be chalked up to the racist system; the evidence of the racist system is the presence of such violence in the first place; to deny that race lies at the root of such incidents makes you a cog in the racist system. The circular logic, protected by an enormous so-called Kafka trap—in which protestations of innocence are treated as proof of guilt—means that systemic racism is subject to no falsification.

And that's precisely the point. Systemic racism is a fundamentalist religious belief. It posits original sin; it posits saints and prophets; it posits its own malevolent god of the gaps. Most of all, it persecutes heretics in the name of a supposedly higher good. To be saved is to declare fealty to radical racial polarization; to be damned is to deny such fealty.

Due Process Is the Opposite of Social Justice

May 5, 2021

It has been two weeks since the conviction of ex-police officer Derek Chauvin for the second- and third-degree murder and second-degree manslaughter of George Floyd. The world has moved on. Politicians breathed a sigh of relief when they heard the verdict; the media quickly moved on to its next manipulated data point in favor of the proposition that American police are systemically racist.

But there were always lingering questions about the verdict. The biggest question was whether Chauvin could have received a fair trial. Jury selection happened while the city of Minneapolis publicized a $27 million settlement with Floyd's family. The judge denied requests for a venue change despite the fact that the trial would take place in a city that had been wracked with riots, looting and burning over Floyd's death. One of the alternate jurors admitted, "I did not want to go through rioting and destruction again, and I was concerned about people coming to my house if they were not happy with the verdict."

A sitting congresswoman traveled to town just before the verdict to suggest the possibility of violence were Chauvin to be acquitted; the president of the United States said openly the day before the verdict came down that he wanted a guilty verdict. Prominent politicians and leftist activists openly stated that without millions marching in the streets, Chauvin probably wouldn't have even stood trial.

Now, there was arguably evidence enough to convict Chauvin on the manslaughter charge. But the two murder charges were questionable, at the very least. There were serious questions to be asked about causation—about whether Floyd died primarily as a result of Chauvin's actions, or whether his underlying drug use and 75% heart arterial blockage was the truer cause of his death. There were also serious questions about the level of force used—when that level of force transformed from the clearly permissible to the feloniously criminal.

And yet, after three weeks of testimony, the jury was out a mere 10 hours, asked zero questions of the judge and came back with a guilty verdict on all counts.

Now it turns out that one of the jurors, Brandon Mitchell, 31, lied during the voir dire process for jury selection. In August 2020, Mitchell appeared in a photo wearing a black T-shirt with the words "Get Your Knee Off Our Necks" as well as a baseball cap with the letters "BLM" (for Black Lives Matter). Mitchell had filled out a 14-page questionnaire in which he explicitly denied having participated in protests over police use of force. He told the judge that he could be an impartial juror.

But this is of little consequence. Our establishment media will surely cover this story as a justifiable, if mildly uncomfortable, afterthought, if they cover it at all. Experts expect that even this evidence will not be enough to reverse the verdict in Chauvin's case.

Perhaps Chauvin deserved to be convicted. That's an open question. He *certainly* deserved the same fair and impartial trial guaranteed every American citizen. It seems likely he didn't receive such due process. But few will care. Chauvin has been convicted, and due process is of little consequence when the safety of the nation relies on conviction. Social justice takes precedence over individual justice these days.

For the Left, Bigotry Is a Tool

March 24, 2021

This week, a white man shot to death eight people in Atlanta-area spas, six of them Asian American. According to Atlanta police, the man said he was targeting brothels and blamed the women for his alleged sex addiction. The gunman stated that he had visited two of the spas before and had planned to drive to Florida and target the pornography industry. So far, there is no evidence that the shooter was motivated by anti-Asian animus, making hate-crime charges unlikely at this point.

Nonetheless, the establishment media and Democratic politicians quickly began reflecting the lie that the shooting was an anti-Asian hate crime, the latest outgrowth of a major uptick in anti-Asian hate crimes—all driven supposedly by "white supremacy." White House press secretary Jen Psaki connected the alleged increase in anti-Asian sentiment to former President Trump, stating that his "calling COVID 'the Wuhan virus'... led... to perceptions of the Asian American community that are inaccurate, unfair." Racial grifter Ibram X. Kendi tweeted: "Locking arms with Asian Americans facing this lethal wave of anti-Asian terror. Their struggle is my struggle. Our struggle is against racism and White supremacist domestic terror." Nikole Hannah-Jones, pseudo-journalist and de facto editor-in-chief at The New York Times, tweeted in solidarity: "I stand with my Asian-American brothers and sisters, just as so many of you have stood with us. I grieve. We must own all of this history—ALL OF IT—and determine to fight for a truly multiracial democracy where we all can be free."

This is cynical politicking at best.

The same sources decrying anti-Asian sentiment have spent years expressing anti-Asian animus in the form of discriminatory college admissions standards: President Biden's administration dropped a discrimination case against Yale University just a month ago, clearly thanks to the administration's position that affirmative action for black students outweighs Asian American success in a pure meritocracy. The same people blaming "white supremacy" for anti-Asian hate crimes have militantly ignored the location of the crimes—largely major metropolitan areas, with a large number of such crimes coming not from white Americans but from black Americans (a plurality of overall violent crimes targeting Asian Americans, according to the Bureau of Justice Statistics, were committed by black Americans in 2018). The same establishment media sources blaming Trump for anti-Asian hate cheer on the active closing of merit-based magnet schools in New York and San Francisco, thanks to those schools' disproportionate Asian American attendance: Hannah-Jones tweeted last year that it was "disingenuous" to talk about "specialized high schools being majority POC" (people of color) when referring to Asian Americans.

Here, then, is how the narrative works, according to the left: No matter the antecedent to any statement, the conclusion must be that America is systemically racist. When we are discussing Asian American economic success, Asian Americans must be treated as beneficiaries of a white supremacist system; when we are talking about hate crimes against Asian Americans, Asian Americans must be treated as people of color victimized by a white supremacist system. When a white person harms Asian Americans, as Trevor Noah explained, intent doesn't matter—animus can be assumed. When a black person harms Asian Americans, as

NBC News reported, "experts say it's important to evaluate each case individually."

All of this is morally base. Anti-Asian animus is anti-Asian animus, whether it comes from woke school administrators or street criminals. To treat such animus differently based solely on the identity of the offender is to make obvious that you simply don't care about anti-Asian animus. For the left, it's just the latest club to wield against the broader American system, facts be damned.

Past Time to Fight Back

April 7, 2021

This week, on the basis of whole-cloth lies, major corporations went to political war with the state of Georgia. The lies at issue revolved around Georgia's new voter law, characterized by both Stacey Abrams and President Joe Biden as a new form of Jim Crow. What do these dastardly new voter restrictions do? They require an ID number to receive an absentee ballot, with language identical to that of federal law; they bar electioneering within 150 feet of a polling place or 25 feet of voters in line, including handing out food or water for partisan purposes; they increase the number of mandatory days of weekend early voting; they preserve some drop boxes that did not exist before the pandemic; they require additional voting machines and election personnel in crowded precincts; they increase voting hours in future elections for the vast majority of counties.

These provisions are similar to the laws in a vast majority of states. That didn't stop Democrats and the media from simply lying about the Georgia voting law. While some in the media did point out that Biden had lied about the law's supposed crackdown on voting hours, nobody in the media treated his "Jim Crow" contentions with the sneering disrespect they so richly deserved. Instead, they simply parroted the line that Republicans were engaged in widespread voter suppression, another lie—a lie far more unsubstantiated than Republican concerns about voter fraud and irregularity.

But the media and Democrats went even further: They bullied corporations into taking positions on the Georgia election law. CBS News put out a headline that trafficked in simple activism: "3 ways companies can help fight Georgia's restrictive new voting law." And companies complied. Coca-Cola, in line with its new Woka-Cola branding, issued a statement deploring an election law the corporation hadn't bothered to lobby against before its passage. Delta issued a statement, too, with CEO Ed Bastian explaining, "I need to make it clear that the final bill is unacceptable and does not match Delta's values." Major League Baseball followed Biden's advice and pulled the All-Star Game out of the state.

So, what should conservatives do?

Many conservatives—myself included—deplore the politics of boycotts. We're not interested in patronizing companies based on political differentiation alone. But if the left is going to hijack the most powerful institutions in America and then weaponize them against voters in red states, conservatives will be left with little choice but to exert counter-pressure.

The only alternative is the formation of alternative companies in every industry. If Coca-Cola wishes to cater to the woke, conservatives will need to build a competitor. Conservatives don't have first-mover advantage in these spaces. But that doesn't alleviate the responsibility to find a different path than funding those who would cut them off at the knees.

The left has politicized everything. The right has avoided that tactic, because it's ugly and divisive. But it's too late to put the genie back in the bottle. It's time for mutually assured destruction. There's only one thing worse than having nuclear weapons: unilateral disarmament. Better to establish mutually assured destruction now and put corporate America on notice that, by stepping into the middle of fraught political debate, it risks just as much blowback from the right as from the left.

The Fight Over Identity

April 14, 2021

America has been wrecked on the shoals of identity.

Identity politics has been characterized casually as a form of tribalism: Americans grouping themselves according to biological or sexual characteristics, in opposition to other groups associated by biological or sexual characteristics. There is certainly truth to the idea that such tribalism has damaged America in extraordinary ways—that tribalism acts as the sort of factionalism the Founding Fathers feared, tearing Americans from one another and forcing them into polarized units to compete against others in a battle over control.

But there is another form of identity politics even more sinister than the sort of tribalism we see so openly today, a form that focuses less on politics than on identity: the redefinition of identity itself.

For thousands of years, human beings established their identities by learning how to adapt to the systems in which they lived, gradually changing those systems for the better after determining the flaws within them. This is how parents traditionally *civilized* children—by adapting them to their civilization.

But as Carl Trueman explains in his masterful book "The Rise and Triumph of the Modern Self," the post-Enlightenment era tore away at the core assumption of such notions of identity. Instead of adapting ourselves to the institutions around us and forming our identity within those institutions, human beings in the West began to locate their identity *within*—to look to their own sense of authenticity as the guide to fulfillment. In this view, identity was not formed in tandem with civilization but in opposition to it. Only by rebelling against the strictures of a surrounding society, by breaking free of convention, could individuals finally achieve fulfillment.

Furthermore, fulfillment would require not merely an interior sense of identity but a sense of identity cheered and celebrated by everyone else. After all, human beings still feel the need for acceptance. To reject someone else's authentic sense of self-identification, therefore, becomes an act of emotional violence.

We have now taken this view to its logical endpoint: total subjectivism, requiring the destruction of any and all conflicting viewpoints or data. Take, for example, a recent New York Times piece applauding the rise of so-called neopronouns. With the explosion of new subjective identities—and the demand that others endorse them—has come a wave of new pronouns. We are no longer talking about biological males demanding that others identify them as "she/her" in contravention of all available objective science. We are talking about people insisting that others call them "kitten/kittenself" or "vamp/vampself." Now, some might find this to be frivolous nonsense disconnected from any true sense of identity. But as The New York Times blithely notes, "what's the difference between an aesthetic and an identity anyway?"

This is saying the quiet part out loud. For decades, those who insist that identity is constructed in opposition to society's rules—rules that must be eliminated in order to achieve human flourishing—have suggested that authentic identity is more than mere aesthetics. But now The Times has given away the show: When you construct identity as a tabula rasa, seeing all history and science as obstacles to happiness, identity quickly flattens into aesthetics. And we are all expected to agree with your sense of aesthetics. (Unless, as The Times notes, you identify as "BLM" or other terms related to Black Lives Matter. In that case, you are encroaching on longstanding areas of sensitivity and must atone.)

When identity becomes pure aesthetics, society completely atomizes. No free society can be rooted in utter subjectivity—someone must enforce silence from the top, bar dissenters and punish those who insist on objective data. And that's precisely what we are seeing from an authoritarian left: an authoritarian left that arrived with the promise of fulfillment and authenticity and has instead delivered emptiness and aesthetic pretension, enforced by institutional fiat.

The Muddled Thinking of 'Antiracism'

June 2, 2021

This week, a clip of America's most prominent racial grifter, Ibram X. Kendi, began making the rounds on Twitter. Kendi, the author of "How to Be an Antiracist," has undoubtedly made a fortune by indicting those who disagree with him as complicit in American racism—and by providing partial absolution to those who repeat his cultish ideas. In one particular clip from a recent interview, however, Kendi was asked to do one very simple thing: to define racism itself. Kendi failed signally in that task. "I would define it as a collection of racist policies that lead to racial inequity that are substantiated by racist ideas," Kendi stated.

The audience laughed out loud.

Kendi then reiterated his definition and added: "And antiracism is pretty simple using the same terms. Antiracism is a collection of antiracist policies leading to racial... equity that are substantiated by antiracist ideas."

This, of course, is utterly nonsensical. No term can be defined by simple reference to the term itself. If someone asked you to define an elephant and you quickly explained that an elephant is, in fact, an animal known as an elephant, you would be adding no new information. If someone asked you to describe anger and you then defined anger as the feeling of being angry, you would leave the listener in serious doubt as to your sanity.

Yet the left not only nods along to this; it champions it. For deep thoughts like Kendi's, CEOs pay millions: Jack Dorsey of Twitter gave Kendi's Center for Antiracist

Research at Boston University $10 million last year; The Vertex Foundation of Vertex Pharmaceuticals is giving Kendi's center $1.5 million over three years; Bank of America has brought in Kendi to deliver his insipid message; The Boston Globe has teamed with Kendi's center to create a new media platform. To date, the Center for Antiracist Research has generated precisely zero research; its website reads, "We are now accepting proposals for our research and policy teams." The center is also accepting applications for its "Antibigotry Convening." And, of course, the center has merchandise, including Antiracist Book Festival face masks (for just $25!).

The goal of many on the left these days is not clarification but obfuscation, particularly on racial issues. Data is not only unnecessary; it's reviled. If the left wishes to promote the argument that racial inequalities are the result of historic injustices, one would hope that someone would bother quantifying to what extent those inequalities are the result of individual decisions versus the result of other factors. If, for example, differential poverty rates by community are highly related to single motherhood—and if single motherhood can only be avoided through personal decision-making—then focusing on historic racism to the exclusion of personal decision-making not only does little good; it does active harm. Yet that is precisely what Kendi proposes—and he calls you racist if you suggest otherwise.

Kendi's solutions are the sorts of solutions the left likes. He has proposed a federal Department of Antiracism with the power to pre-clear "all local, state and federal public policies to ensure they won't yield racial inequity, monitor those policies, investigate private racist policies when racial inequity surfaces, and monitor public officials for expressions of racist ideas." In other words, it's authoritarian dictatorship to establish Kendi's vaguely defined antiracism.

The left embraces this loose thinking because it promotes a broader agenda: blaming institutions broadly for all problems and then remolding those institutions. In this task, obfuscation becomes profoundly important, lest Americans recognize that in a free America, the best path toward alleviating inequity is individual rights rather than a top-down rewriting of American society.

The Movement Against Critical Race Theory Is Deeply Necessary

June 23, 2021

According to the establishment media, critical race theory, or CRT, is a distraction. It is a right-wing smear. It is a conservative attempt to quash the dark side of American history. Most of all, according to the establishment media, you must never—ever—pay attention to the infusion of CRT into the nation's institutions of power. According to MSNBC's Chuck Todd, controversy over CRT is a "creation... It keeps people watching or it keeps people clicking." According to CNN's Bakari Sellers, CRT is just "America's history." According to The Washington Post's Jonathan Capehart, those who criticize CRT are merely attempting to prevent "us from learning our history."

Critical race theory, of course, is not America's actual history. It is a perverse worldview, unsupportable by the evidence, in which all of America's key institutions are inextricably rooted in white supremacy; it is an activist campaign demanding the destruction of those institutions. The founders of CRT have written as much. According to CRT founders Richard Delgado and Jean Stefancic, CRT is founded on two key premises: that "racism is ordinary, not aberrational—'normal science,' the usual way society does business, the common, everyday experience of most people of color in this country"; second, that "our system of white-over-color ascendancy serves important purposes, both psychic and material." This means, according to Delgado and Stefancic, that "racism is difficult to cure or address" and that a formal commitment to legal equality on the basis of color-blindness is merely a guise for further discrimination. Furthermore, CRT founders say that whites are unable to understand racism, and that "minority status... brings with it a presumed competence to speak about race and racism."

CRT therefore holds that racism is embedded deeply in American life, unconsciously into white American psyches, and that it is impossible for white Americans to understand their own racism or that of the system, let alone to remove it. The only solution: tearing away the only systems that have ever provided widespread liberty and prosperity. As fellow CRT founder Derrick Bell wrote, "The whole liberal worldview of private rights and public sovereignty mediated by the rule of law needed to be exploded."

CRT isn't merely a tool of legal analysis, either, as many of its dishonest defenders claim. Delgado and Stefancic are clear: "Although CRT began as a movement in the law, it has rapidly spread beyond that discipline. Today, many in the field of education consider themselves critical race theorists... Political scientists ponder voting strategies coined by critical race theorists... Unlike some academic disciplines, critical race theory contains an activist dimension."

So, what has CRT accomplished? The near-complete subjugation of our higher educational system, which now traffics regularly in CRT-related theories; the corruption of our establishment media, who parrot the anti-Americanism of CRT as "just history"; the infusion of CRT into nearly every area of the government, under the Biden-esque Newspeak of "equity." And yet, if Americans notice this—if Americans lobby school boards to bar indoctrination in the cultish nonsense of CRT—these institutional actors tell those Americans that there is nothing to see.

The grassroots pushback against CRT is rooted in the

best of the American tradition: a rejection of racial essentialism in favor of individualism, an enthusiastic endorsement of agency rather than determinism, a willingness to stand united against tribalism. We all ought to fight those who have hijacked and weaponized our institutions against all of these traditionally American ideals. Anything less would be an abdication of the trust we have been given—a trust that has resulted in liberty, equality and prosperity beyond imagining for nearly all of human history.

Yes, It's Ungrateful to Turn Your Back on the National Anthem

June 30, 2021

This week, heretofore nearly anonymous hammer thrower Gwen Berry made international headlines when, during the podium ceremony for winning bronze in an Olympic trial, she turned away from the United States flag as the national anthem played. The anthem wasn't played for her, or for the other competitors in the hammer throw; every day during the trials, a pre-scheduled anthem went out over the sound system.

Berry turned 90 degrees from the flag, stood with her hand on her hip, and glared directly into the camera. It was a deliberate provocation and a deliberate attempt to raise her own profile. "I feel like it was a setup," she later complained, "and they did it on purpose."

Actually, Berry just saw an opportunity to maximize her profile, and she seized it with alacrity. In the United States, there's far more money to be made and fame to be achieved by spurning the American flag and the national anthem than by embracing it: Colin Kaepernick makes millions because he failed as a quarterback but succeeded as a self-aggrandizing symbol of supposed racial bravery. Meanwhile, the thousands of athletes with track records superior to either Kaepernick's or Berry's who stand for the national anthem remain anonymous.

That's because America currently rewards an entitled sense of grievance. Most Americans know little about foreign countries; they somehow believe that the United States is inferior, or that the prosperity, health and free lifestyle to which they have become accustomed is the global and historic norm.

It most assuredly is not.

While Berry was protesting the national anthem, the Chinese government was busy arresting the editor of the pro-democracy Hong Kong newspaper Apple Daily. That arrest came on the heels of the arrest of one of Apple Daily's columnists for "conspiring to collude with foreign countries or foreign forces to endanger national security." While Berry was protesting the national anthem, the Taliban was busy spreading like a metastasizing cancer over Afghanistan, preparing its new subjects for the tender mercies of brutal Islamist rule. While Berry was protesting the national anthem during an event at which she threw heavy objects for sport, billions of people were living in absolute privation the world over.

None of this means that the shortcomings of America should be ignored. But to protest the flag or the national anthem as particular symbols of grievance is to demonstrate full-scale your own ignorance and ingratitude. "I'm here to represent those who died due to systemic racism," Berry said. But she herself is an excellent indicator of just how much promise America holds for its citizens. She grew up in the home of her grandmother, with 13 people in the house; she had a baby out of wedlock at 15 and then earned a college scholarship. She got two jobs and helped support her extended family. Now, she's going to the Olympics. And presumably, there, she will turn her back on the flag and the national anthem if she makes it to the podium.

In doing so, she'll become a hero to millions. She'll get richer; she'll get more famous. Perhaps, like pseudo-Marxist Patrisse Cullors of Black Lives Matter, she'll buy herself a few houses; maybe, like Kaepernick, she'll make the cover of Sports Illustrated. Like self-declared Marxist

Cullors, who currently owns three separate houses worth over $1.5 million each, Berry is in it for the attention and the profit. Yesterday, nobody had heard of her. Today, everybody has. It's that simple.

One thing is certain, however: Those who spend their days championing their own ingratitude at a society that gives them extraordinary opportunities—opportunities unavailable to nearly all humans for nearly all of human history, and unavailable to most people on the planet right now—aren't likely to live happier lives. And they're unlikely to make their nations better, either.

Stop Surrendering Education to the Radical Left

July 7, 2021

This Independence Day, a poll from Issues & Insights revealed that only 36% of adults aged 18-24 said they were "proud to be American," compared with 86% of those over the age of 65. This shouldn't be surprising. America's children have been raised in a system dedicated to the proposition that America itself is evil, a repository of discrimination and bigotry, a country founded in sin and steeped in cruelty.

This week, for example, the National Education Association, the single largest teachers union in the country, passed a resolution pledging to "Share and publicize… information already available on critical race theory (CRT)"; "Provide an already-created, in-depth, study that critiques empire, white supremacy, anti-Blackness, anti-Indigeneity, racism, patriarchy, cisheteropatriarchy, capitalism, ableism, anthropocentrism, and other forms of power and oppression at the intersections of our society"; and "Join with Black Lives Matter at School and the Zinn Education Project to call for a rally this year on October 14—George Floyd's birthday—as a national day of action to teach lessons about structural racism and oppression." Meanwhile, the American Federation of Teachers is hosting radical grifter Ibram X. Kendi, who preaches on behalf of overt racial discrimination.

Now Americans are banding together to fight back against the indoctrination of its children. States have begun to ban the indoctrination of CRT in schools, for example.

But some thinkers are fighting back, suggesting that such content standards undermine the notion of a liberal education. In the pages of The New York Times, for example, a bipartisan group of thinkers excoriate such legislation as "un-American." They argue, essentially, that the educational mission of "helping turn students into well-informed and discerning citizens" is undermined by such restrictions.

But this completely misreads both the purpose of American education and the state of American education. First, the purpose of public education is to create "well-informed and discerning citizens." But "citizens" is a specific word with a specific definition. According to Aristotle, a "good citizen" is a person who upholds the Constitution of his particular polis. If we teach our students to be bad citizens in the Aristotelian sense—citizens who disparage the polis with lies, who engage in tribal politicking rather than civic friendship, who insist that truth be subsumed in favor of intersectional sensitivities—we will wind up as a country with no future.

Second, American public education has all-too-often become a tool of those who wish to produce anti-citizens: those who wish to tear down the systems in the name of some higher or lower purpose. No society can survive this in the long term. K-12 public education was not designed to be a free-for-all; standards and practices must be established. The only question is whose standards and whose practices. For the past several decades, the answer seems to be the radical left's standards, undermining key American principles like individual rights and equality before the law in favor of a utopian redistribution of outcome based on group identity. It is one thing to discuss the ideological perversion of CRT in order to combat it; it is another thing to indoctrinate in its central tenets. Our education system is currently far more likely to do the latter than the former.

That must stop. Good citizens have an obligation to stop it. Whether that happens through the mechanisms of civil rights lawsuits or through the mechanisms of local school board elections or through the mechanism of state legislation—all appropriate tools when it comes to defining how our children ought to be educated at public expense— radical indoctrination of our children must stop. To do anything less would be un-American.

The Narrative Is the Priority

November 17, 2021

According to the media, Kyle Rittenhouse was a white supremacist. According to the media, Kyle Rittenhouse was an active shooter. According to the media, Kyle Rittenhouse was a murderer.

In reality, he was none of these.

Kyle Rittenhouse was a 17-year-old young man who went to Kenosha, Wisconsin, in order to protect businesses and administer medical aid to those who needed it. He was chased down by Joseph Rosenbaum, a 36-year-old convicted child molester; he shot Rosenbaum when Rosenbaum grabbed for his gun. He was then chased down by Anthony Huber, 26, a man convicted of two felony counts of strangulation and suffering after pulling a knife on his brother and grandmother and choking his brother; Rittenhouse shot Huber when Huber tried to slam his skateboard into Rittenhouse's head. Finally, Gaige Grosskreutz, 27, a member of a radical Antifa offshoot, approached Rittenhouse with a pistol in his hand; Rittenhouse shot him in the biceps.

All of this was on tape. It was verified by witness testimony and physical evidence.

Yet Rittenhouse was brought to trial anyway.

He was brought to trial because his case became the center of a political firestorm. In September 2020, Joe Biden featured Rittenhouse in an ad decrying then-President Donald Trump's supposed sympathy for white supremacists. Members of the Left declared that Rittenhouse was a stand-in for American racism, despite the fact that all three of the people Rittenhouse shot were white. Even after the prosecution presented its case—a case so weak that the prosecution's own witnesses ended up supporting Rittenhouse's self-defense case—members of the media continued to maintain that an exoneration for Rittenhouse would be yet another stain on America's racial record.

Meanwhile, last week, we learned that the Department of Justice had indicted one Igor Danchenko, a Russia analyst who worked with Christopher Steele on the infamous Steele dossier—a collection of bizarre misinformation about Trump treated as blockbuster material by the media. Danchenko, it is alleged, concealed that one of his informational sources was a Democratic Party operative close with the Clinton family. This means that Steele, at the behest of Hillary Clinton's hired guns at Fusion GPS, gathered false information from Clinton allies, and laundered it into a report—and then Clinton's team handed the Steele report over to the FBI, which promptly used it as the basis for a FISA warrant against Carter Page, a member of the Trump campaign. The Clinton campaign then used the FBI investigation of Team Trump as a campaign point.

The media, of course, went right along with all of this. When the Steele dossier went public, members of the media treated it as though it were verified and credible. As Bill Grueskin, former academic dean at Columbia Journalism School, writes, "some reporters simply didn't like or trust Mr. Trump and didn't want to appear to be on his side."

Jussie Smollett was not attacked by MAGA-hatted white thugs; the media treated his initial story with complete credulity. Christine Blasey Ford provided no supporting evidence for her allegations against Brett Kavanaugh; the media treated her as a groundbreaking heroine. The high schoolers of Covington Catholic did not mock a Native American man; the media treated them as evil white supremacists. Jacob Blake was not wrongfully shot by police; the media treated his shooting as a case of systemic police racism. No evidence was ever presented that Derek Chauvin killed George Floyd based on race; his case nonetheless became the point of the spear in our "national conversation" about racism.

How many facts will die at the hands of media-crafted narratives? As many as need to die in order to achieve political utopia for the Left. As David Burge suggested years ago on Twitter, "Journalism is about covering important stories. With a pillow, until they stop moving."

Reality Remains Undefeated

November 24, 2021

This week, a 39-year-old black man in Waukesha, Wisconsin, plowed a maroon Ford Escape into a Christmas parade of children and older women. Five people were killed and another 48 were injured. The motive of the suspect is unknown; if the media have their way, it will remain that way. The media apparently only care about why suspects commit violent acts when motives can be credited to their political enemies.

There is one thing we do know: the suspect should not have been on the street. He had a rap sheet longer than the first five books of the Bible. His latest alleged crime took place on Nov. 5, when he was charged with resisting an officer, bail jumping, recklessly endangering safety, disorderly conduct and battery. First, he allegedly slammed the mother of his child with his fist, and then ran her over—wait for it—in a maroon Ford Escape. He was released on Friday… on $1,000 bail. Two days later, he ran his vehicle over innocent victims.

The Milwaukee County District Attorney's Office has now opened an investigation into the low bail. But we already know just why the bail process allowed the suspect back out onto the street: equity demanded it. In May 2015, Jeffrey Toobin wrote in The New Yorker about "The Milwaukee Experiment." The piece was a long, sycophantic love letter to John Chisholm, the District Attorney of Milwaukee County, who had embraced criminal justice policies geared toward rectifying "the racial imbalance in American prisons." According to one of Chisholm's admirers, "Chisholm stuck his neck out there and started saying that prosecutors should also be judged by their success in reducing mass incarceration and achieving racial equality."

Not reducing crime. Reducing the number of people in jail—and more particularly, the number of black Americans in jail. Chisholm himself admitted the costs of his policies in 2007: "Is there going to be an individual I divert, or I put into a treatment program, who's going to go out and kill somebody? You bet. Guaranteed. It's guaranteed to happen."

Chisholm, of course, was right.

San Francisco proved the same point this week when large, roving gangs began looting high-end stores. On Friday night, San Francisco's Union Square witnessed a massive group of looters smashing and grabbing at a Louis Vuitton store; meanwhile, thieves congregated to steal product in Walnut Creek, Pleasanton, Hayward and San Jose. None of this ought to be a surprise. San Francisco District Attorney Chesa Boudin announced that he would end "mass incarceration" and cash bail; he stopped prosecuting shoplifting cases—in 2020, just 44% of shoplifting cases were prosecuted.

The result: stores are closing down in San Francisco thanks to the automatic surcharge of people stealing their product from the shelves.

Reality with regard to criminality isn't all that complicated: when you free criminals unjustifiably in a misguided attempt to achieve "group equity," innocents suffer. When you take cops off the street, freeing criminals to work their will, innocents suffer. When you refuse to prosecute crime, criminals spot an opportunity.

Voters can either continue to deny reality and pay the price, or they can wake up to the simple fact that reality always wins. Until they do the latter, the criminals—and the politicians who enable them—will be the only winners.

The Left's War With Biological Reality

December 8, 2021

As the Supreme Court determines whether to preserve the Court-created "right to abortion" under Roe v. Wade, those on the feminist Left have gone into full-blown panic mode. Women's rights, they insist, will implode without granting women the ability to abort their children; only that ability can equalize the natural inequalities of biology, by which women are saddled with the burden of childbearing and child rearing.

This war with biology is central to the Left's definition of autonomy itself. In the pages of The New York Times, Democratic activist Elizabeth Spiers made this perfectly clear in arguing that abortion ought to be considered the moral alternative to adoption. "When I awoke," she writes, "my son would wake up shortly after and I'd feel him turning and stretching, or less pleasantly, jamming his precious little foot into what felt like my cervix. This is one of the paradoxes of pregnancy: something alien is usurping your body and sapping you of nutrition and energy, but you're programmed to gleefully enable it and you become desperately protective of it. It's a kind of biological brainwashing."

Biological brainwashing.

The same people who maintain that your biology dictates that you can be a man in a woman's body and that this represents not gender dysphoria—truly, a form of biological brainwashing—but an objective reality to which all of society should conform also argue that biology creates morally unjust connections between mother and child. As

Spiers says, "biological brainwashing... occurs during pregnancy"; mothers cannot "simply choose not to bond with a child she's gestating solely on the basis that she is not ready to be a mother or believes that she is unable to provide for the child." This means that women should consider killing the child rather than putting it up for adoption.

The language of "biological brainwashing" doesn't stop with the bond between mother and child. This week, Rep. Alexandria Ocasio-Cortez, D-N.Y., the spectacularly dull Instagram star, characterized opposition to abortion as the legalization of "forced birth." In her view, biology itself is an imposition on women (the Left conveniently drops its Orwellian "birthing people" lingo when abortion is at stake); ending a pregnancy by killing an unborn child is a restoration of the natural order.

Precisely the opposite is true, of course. A predictable result of sex—in fact, the evolutionary biological purpose of sex—is procreation. The process by which conception results in birth is continuous and natural. Interfering in that process by forced killing of an unborn human life is definitionally unnatural.

But so is the entire Leftist worldview by which true autonomy represents an opposition between spirit and flesh. According to the Left, any check on our ambitions— even a check provided by the reality of biology—must be overcome in order to establish true equality of opportunity. Women are different than men in biology; therefore, biology must be opposed.

The results of this madness are obvious: men and women alienated from themselves, angry at the realities of life, willing to forgo perhaps the greatest joy of existence—the perpetuation of the human species through the birth of children. But other civilizations are not so suicidal. While we amuse ourselves to death, solipsistically focused on our own subjective sense of autonomy, other civilizations recognize, at the very least, that biology is an inescapable reality. Those civilizations that best conform to the beauty of that reality will thrive. Those that do not will destroy themselves.

Whoopi Goldberg Says the Holocaust Wasn't About Targeting Jews. Here's Why That Matters.

February 2, 2022

This week, former award-winning actress and highly decorated blowhard Whoopi Goldberg made a fool of herself. This came as no surprise; Goldberg does that quite regularly on "The View." The good news for Goldberg is that no one notices—trying to identify which fatuous host takes the cake for most imbecilic comment on any given day is an exercise in multivariate calculus, so Goldberg often tends to meld into the wallpaper of daftness.

But on Monday, Goldberg truly stood out.

Discussing an obscure Tennessee school board deciding to remove the Pulitzer Prize-winning graphic novel "Maus" from a Holocaust unit for eighth-graders, Goldberg launched into an explanation of the Holocaust dazzling in both its ignorance and its malignity.

Joy Behar, the usual top contender for the Crown of Idiocy, led off by explaining that the Tennessee school board members "don't like history that makes white people look bad." Then Goldberg got going: "Maybe. This is white people doing it to white people. Y'all go fight amongst yourselves."

This comment would have been insanely insulting, in and of itself: Here was Goldberg, referring to Nazis and Jews as "white people doing it to white people." But Goldberg was just getting started. "If we're going to do this," Goldberg said, "let's be truthful about it because the Holocaust isn't about race. No. It's not about race." Behar correctly said, "They considered Jews a different race." But

Goldberg would not tolerate the dissent: "It's not about race. It's not about race… It's about man's inhumanity to man. That's what it's about."

At this point, Ana Navarro attempted to intervene and stop the crazy train. "But it's about white supremacy," Navarro said. "It's about going after Jews and gypsies." No, said Goldberg. "These are two white groups of people… You're missing the point. The minute you turn it into race, it goes down this alley. Let's talk about it for what it is. It's how people treat each other. It's a problem. It doesn't matter if you are black or white because black, white, Jews, Italians, everybody eats each other."

The asininity cannot be overstated here. It is absolutely clear that the Nazis targeted Jews as a race; Hitler wasn't exactly hiding the ball when he stated in "Mein Kampf": "Is not their very existence founded on one great lie, namely, that they are a religious community, whereas in reality they are a race?" Hitler repeatedly referred to the Jews as a race of parasites, and targeted Jews on the basis of ethnicity rather than religious adherence.

The question must be asked, then: What, precisely, did Goldberg think she was doing? The answer is that she believed she was upholding the intersectional theory of race and racism. That theory holds that society is structured in a hierarchy of victimized and victimizing groups; that groups that are disproportionately successful are victimizers, and that groups that are disproportionately less successful are victimized. Jews are disproportionately successful; thus, they are white. And, intersectional theory posits, racism is not defined as a belief that any other race is superior or inferior to another; instead, racism means—as the Anti-Defamation League recently defined it—"the marginalization and/or oppression of people of color based on a socially constructed racial hierarchy that privileges white people."

These two concepts, taken in tandem, mean that Jews cannot be considered victims of antisemitism. They are highly successful; they are white. Thus, they cannot be members of a victimized minority. This is why the mainstream Left is so reluctant to recognize the antisemitism of Hamas (Democratic Rep. Jamaal Bowman, for example, condemned Israel for defending itself against rocket attacks by Hamas by decrying "Black and brown bodies being brutalized and murdered"); it is why the mainstream Left is complicit in the lie that the only true antisemitism springs from white supremacists, ignoring actual acts of Jew-hatred by members of minority populations. The intersectional Left's conspiracy theory—that a cabal of white victimizers (including Jews, and now, Asians) control society for its own benefit—inherently crosses streams with antisemitism.

Goldberg's comments aren't an aberration. They're merely the latest iteration of a pernicious and perverse theory of power in politics—a conspiracy theory about groups that succeed and the systems in which they succeed.

The Attack on Joe Rogan Is an Attack on Dissent

February 9, 2022

Joe Rogan must be stopped.

This is the consensus from all of the wisest and most compassionate voices in our society. According to the White House, Spotify should not merely lead off Rogan's COVID-19-centric episodes with a content warning; according to press secretary Jen Psaki, "our view is that it is a positive step, but that there is more that can be done." According to CNN's Brian Stelter, host of the ironically named "Reliable Sources": "He is now apologizing. And we're going to find out if that's enough for Spotify, the company that has an exclusive distribution deal with him." Has-been rocker Neil Young agrees; he, along with some other washed-up old hippie musicians, has taken his music off of Spotify to protest Rogan.

What was Rogan's great sin? To hear the media tell it, his great sin was COVID-19 "misinformation." Now, this is a rather vague charge, given the fact that our public health authorities have informed us over the course of the past two years that lockdowns were effective, cloth masks worked, masking of children was necessary, vaccines prevented transmission, natural immunity was inferior to vaccine immunity, and the virus could not have originated with a Chinese lab leak—all pieces of misinformation later reversed. Nonetheless, Rogan vowed to become more informed and to have on more diverse guests with regard to COVID-19 and vaccines.

When Spotify didn't deplatform Rogan over *that* charge, the rationale for his demanded deplatforming morphed: now Rogan was a racist for saying the N-word while quoting rap lyrics years ago. After a Left-wing activist group promoted a compendium video of Rogan using such language, Rogan apologized again. But apologies aren't the point. No one actually thinks Rogan is a racist. For the radical Left, you either become a tool in their arsenal or you become an object lesson. And Rogan has now become an object lesson.

He has become an object lesson for two main reasons. First, Rogan has steadfastly refused to toe the party line with regard to President Joe Biden; ire broke out against Rogan in 2020 for the crime of noting that Biden appeared "mentally compromised" in the middle of an election that the media had declared a turning point in the future of democracy. Second, Rogan has hosted guests who do not simply repeat the nostrums of the Left on a wide variety of issues. That's why the Left has demanded that Spotify remove old episodes of his show entirely: Alternative voices must not be heard, and Rogan has the unfortunate habit of talking to such voices for hours at a time and letting them say their piece.

There are several takeaways from the Rogan dust-up.

First, corporate overlords are absolutely gutless. CEO Daniel Ek believed that picking up the exclusive license to Rogan's show would increase listenership and advertising dollars; he was clearly blindsided by the blowback, to the extent that he issued a mewling letter to the company's woke interns begging their forgiveness for their hurt feelings.

Second, the media are not interested in freedom of speech as a principle. They're interested in freedom of speech for themselves and no one else. It's been fascinating to watch the evolution of our treasured Journalismers (TM) from guardians of the First Amendment to attack dogs on behalf of Big Tech censorship of their perceived enemies.

Third, apologizing to insincere radical Left alligators is always a mistake. Their goal is not a conversation. Their goal is destruction. If they find you useful, they may allow you to become Reek to their House Bolton; if they don't, you become Ned Stark to their Joffrey.

Rogan will survive all of this. Perhaps Spotify ends up paying him a bag of cash to leave, and he takes his audience and goes elsewhere, tanking Spotify's stock price on his way out the door. That would be precisely what Spotify deserves for their cowardice. But no matter what happens, the lesson will be learned by those who don't have Rogan's audience: shut up or face the whirlwind. And most will shut up.

The War On Parents Continues

February 23, 2022

In September 2020, January Littlejohn went to pick up her 13-year-old daughter from middle school. Littlejohn is a stay-at-home mother to three children and a licensed mental health counselor in Florida. So when her daughter informed her that the school administration had begun encouraging her to identify as transgender, Littlejohn was shocked.

Littlejohn's daughter told her that school administrators had asked her about changing her name, which restroom she wished to use, and whether she wanted to sleep with boys or girls on school trips. According to the district, parents were to be cut out of the loop unless the 13-year-old gave her consent to their involvement; the district stated that "outing a student, especially to parents, can be very dangerous to the student's health and well-being."

So, to be clear, the school would have had to phone Littlejohn for permission to administer an Advil; presumably if Littlejohn's daughter had been suffering from depression or anxiety in school, parents would have been notified as well. But the school purposefully avoided telling Littlejohn about her daughter considering whether she was a boy or a girl, and all the attendant acts toward social transition—all of which is often followed by hormone replacement or surgery. The school not only felt no duty to keep Littlejohn in the loop, but they also treated Littlejohn as an enemy to her own child.

This, indeed, is the mentality of an enormous swath of the social Left these days. Florida is now considering a bill, the Parental Rights in Education bill, that would restrict primary schools from indoctrinating children on matters of sexual orientation or gender identity and would require schools to inform parents about minors who begin identifying as LGBTQ in school. None of this should be controversial: Parents have always been and will always be the adults with the most stake in their children. It is parents who care most about their children, not school administrators; it is parents who shape the values and choices of their children.

But that's precisely what the Left hates. To the Left, parents are the enemy. Without any evidence of abuse—or even any allegations of abuse—the Left now states that forcing schools to provide transparency to parents about their children is a form of abuse. As California Gov. Gavin Newsom put it, telling schools to keep parents in the loop is "nothing short of a state-sponsored intimidation of LGBTQ children. It will put kids—who are already navigating stress—in physical and psychological danger."

The Left, instead, wishes to teach its own version of sexual morality and gender identity to small children, without the messy intervention of parents. It is indeed that simple. And, of course, this has an impact. It is designed to have an impact. There is a reason that, according to Gallup, just 0.8% of those born before 1946 identify as LGBT, and that just 2.6% of those born between 1946 and 1964 do—but that fully 20.8% of all those born between 1997 and 2003 identify as LGBT. That reason is not evolutionary biology making a radical turn, or even additional tolerance for such activity. The reason is that our society has decided that belief in traditional standards with regard to both sex and sexual activity must be fought tooth and nail. Any parent who holds to those standards must be treated as a threat—not to the children they care about far more than activists do, but to the new standard.

Now, perhaps the new standard is somehow superior to the old. If the Left wishes to make that case, they can certainly do so. But the Left does not have the right to hijack the minds of children and then weaponize them against their parents using public dollars, all the while pretending that such activity is actually altruism on behalf of children. It isn't. It's cruel to children and cruel to parents.

The Slap Heard Around the World

March 30, 2022

  This week, Will Smith—perhaps the most bankable star of his generation—won an Oscar for Best Actor for "King Richard." But that wasn't why he made headlines. He made headlines because during the Academy Awards ceremony, comedian Chris Rock told a joke about Smith's wife, Jada Pinkett Smith. Jada, it seems, suffers from alopecia; Rock, presumably not knowing about her condition, made a joke about her starring in "G.I. Jane 2," a nod to her closely shaven head. Initially, Will Smith laughed. Then he glanced around and saw Jada was upset.

  At which point he got up, strode to the stage, and proceeded to slap Rock directly across the face.

  Then he sat down again.

  Rock, for his part, tried to play off the situation as a joke. But Will Smith wasn't letting it go. Instead, he began screaming at Rock: "Keep my wife's name out ya f---ing mouth!" Rock replied, "Wow, dude, it was a 'G.I. Jane' joke." To which Smith repeated, screaming, "Keep my wife's name out ya f---ing mouth!" Which, presumably, would make Rock the first man to whom Smith had ever uttered such a sentiment, given the couple's stated dedication to their open marriage.

  Suffice it to say, it was perhaps the oddest incident in nationally televised history. The only rivals might have been Justin Timberlake ripping off Janet Jackson's top to reveal a pasty at the Super Bowl XXXVIII halftime show, or the live OJ Simpson car chase during the NBA Finals. But this event was even odder, given the utterly sudden nature of the assault. Rock, after all, was hired to lightly roast actors. Will Smith was there to pick up his first Oscar. And the whole thing devolved into actual violence.

It's easy to brush off the event as yet another disposably silly celebrity moment. It would be easier if Rep. Ayanna Pressley, D-Mass., hadn't immediately tweeted (and then deleted), "Thank you #WillSmith Shout out to all the husbands who defend their wives living with alopecia in the face of daily ignorance & insults." Or if Rep. Jamaal Bowman, D-N.Y., hadn't tweeted, "Teachable Moment: Don't joke about a Black Woman's hair." Or if the entire Academy Awards audience hadn't given Smith a standing ovation a few moments later. Or if there hadn't been widespread support for Smith's slap online, thanks to the now-common belief that verbal insults constitute a form of violence to which violence is an acceptable—indeed, commendable—response.

The social compact by which verbiage and violence remain strictly separated is a delicate one. For most of human history, words were treated as punishable by physical response—dueling was commonplace in societies for centuries, familial retaliation for insult was regular, and wars were even fought over verbal slights. But over time, civilized people traded away the privilege of personal use of force in favor of rules; truly offensive words could sometimes meet with social disapproval or even ostracization, but certainly not violence.

Now we seem to be reversing the trend. The entire theory of "microaggressions" suggests that if you are offended, it is because someone has "aggressed" against you—and aggression requires response. To deny someone's preferred pronouns is now an act of "erasure" amounting to violence, since the person so slighted might feel damaged in their sense of worth or authenticity. Once we reconnect the severed link between words and violence, civilization will begin to break down.

We can hope that Will Smith's slap remains an aberration; a country in which comedians are regularly assaulted for making jokes will soon be a rather humorless place. But unless Americans are willing to reestablish the hard barrier between words and violence, we will become a far more silent and far more violent nation.

The Left Is the Culture War Aggressor

April 6, 2022

Last week, reporter Christopher Rufo released footage of top Disney employees vowing to inject their radical LGBTQ agenda into children's programming. Disney producer Latoya Raveneau told an all-hands meeting that her team works to push a "not-at-all-secret gay agenda" in programming aimed at kids and sought to add "queerness" to such content. Disney corporate president Karey Burke announced that she was the mother of "one transgender child and one pansexual child" and that she would try to achieve a quota system whereby half of all Disney characters would be LGBTQ or people of color. Disney diversity and inclusion manager Vivian Ware stated that Disney's beloved theme parks would be eliminating any mention of "ladies and gentlemen" or "boys and girls."

This prompted a well-deserved firestorm for the Mouse House. Disney has long been Left-wing on social issues—but in the aftermath of ginned-up controversy surrounding Florida's Parental Rights in Education bill, which protects small children from indoctrination on sexual orientation and gender identity, an angry coterie of employees pushed management to signal fealty even harder. So Disney's brass did, announcing that they opposed the Florida bill and then turning over the company to its most radical contingent.

And people reacted. #BoycottDisney began to trend on social media. We at the Daily Wire committed to spending $100 million to develop children's content that would be safe for kids—content dedicated to traditional values, where parents wouldn't have to worry about prescreening content for messages about nonbinary 5-year-olds.

The Left, caught with its hand in the kiddie jar, immediately swiveled and accused the Right of initiating this culture war. Michelle Goldberg of The New York Times lamented that she felt terrible for Raveneau, who, after all, was just "step(ping) up to defend the company's queer friendliness, only to become a national object of right-wing fury and disgust," and whose injection of LGBTQ propaganda into children's content was "sweetly anodyne." CNN hosted Washington Post transgender columnist Charlotte Clymer, adding the chyron "LGBT COMMUNITY LATEST TO BE CAUGHT IN CULTURE WAR." The takeaway, according to the social Left, is that anyone who defends traditionalism in child-rearing—or anyone who simply doesn't want children turned into targets of sexual propagandizing—is the true cultural aggressor.

This is a transparent lie. And it's a lie that won't redound to the benefit of those who seek radical change. If they wish to pose the rubric of gay rights against parental rights, gay rights are likely to suffer. If they wish to suggest that LGBTQ freedom extends to teachers initiating children into sexual conversations without parental permission, parents are unlikely to go along for the ride. For decades, the social Left has made inroads by arguing that they simply want to be left alone. The Right, by contrast, has argued that the Left's agenda is far broader, that the Left demands cultural celebration of its sexual mores and that it will stop at nothing to remake society in order to achieve its narcissistic goals. Disney's latest foray into the culture wars proves that the Right was correct, that the Left's stated agenda was a lie and that its "not-at-all-secret" agenda targeted the most vulnerable Americans.

Disney shows no signs of backing away from the extremism its all-hands meeting unmasked before the world. And other corporations are following Disney's lead, pushing wild Left advocacy instead of catering to the broadest possible market. For too long, Americans have planted their heads firmly in the sand, hoping that the forces of the free market would militate against the cultural hijacking of corporate institutions. Instead, corporations built by entrepreneurs have been hijacked by woke employees and a feckless managerial class. The blowback will be real, and it should be real. And if that means parents swearing off Mickey Mouse, increasingly they will.

The Anarchic Philosophy Behind 'LGBTQI+ Pride Month'

June 1, 2022

June marks LGBTQI+ Pride Month—a month honoring those who are "lesbian, gay, bisexual, transgender, queer and intersex." This ever-expanding rubric revolves around a particular value system entirely embraced by the modern Left: the notion that a person's core identity ought to lie not in the relationship between individual desires and societal duties, but instead ought to revolve around a subjective sense of self, unverifiable by the world at large and justified against all societal roles and rules.

President Joe Biden has said as much from the White House. In a proclamation urging Americans to "wave their flags of pride high"—it is worth noting that an entire side of the political aisle in the United States now finds the so-called pride flag far less controversial than the American flag itself—Biden stated, "This month, we remind the LGBTQI+ community that they are loved and cherished. My administration sees you for who you are—deserving of dignity, respect and support."

Of course, seeing people for who they are typically requires some sort of objective standard; it is literally impossible to see someone for who he is based on his own internal self-perception. This means that Biden is using perfectly Orwellian euphemisms to say that we all ought to validate the self-perception of any he, she, xe or catself.

This perspective is absolutely incoherent. Ironically, this incoherence is exposed by the conflict between the different letters within the alphabet soup of the supposedly sexually marginalized. The case for tolerance of lesbian and gay Americans used to be that biological drives should not be regulated by society at large, because such drives were inborn and innate; that idea at least had the merit of internal consistency. Now, however, that idea has been jettisoned for its logical opposite, the belief that biology has no hold on us whatsoever, and that we ought to be free to define ourselves in opposition to our own biology, changing our gender and sexual orientation at will. Homosexual orientation relies on the continued distinction between the sexes—after all, why prefer males or females if those sexes are mere social constructs? Transgenderism relies on the absolute malleability of sex. This is the reason that so-called TERFs—"trans-exclusionary radical feminists"—are so bewildered by the suddenly mainstream view that women's rights ought to be extended to biological men.

And yet here we are, told by the White House that we must ignore the internal contradictions of Left-wing sexual ideology, and simply pretend the incoherence away. We are told that we ought to stand for women's rights by the same people who insist that Lia Thomas is a woman; we are told that one need not be a biological female to be a lesbian; we are told that biology dictates behavior, but that biology must never be used as an identifier. None of this makes one whit of sense. But we ought to be proud of it, because after all, it liberates us to celebrate our inner sense of authenticity, free of society's strictures.

There is only one problem, of course: this sort of illogic quickly devolves into anarchy. There is no way to speak coherently with one another absent objective meaning, let alone to reach consensus. Suggesting that the world at large owes each of us validation for our innermost desires is a recipe for complete chaos. Unity can only come from opposition to something—and in this case, that means opposition to tradition, institutions and the roles that actually facilitate human flourishing.

Roe v. Wade Is History, but the Abortion Debate Reveals Rot at America's Center

June 29, 2022

This week, the Supreme Court of the United States issued a ruling overdue by some five decades, striking down Roe v. Wade (1973) and its constitutionally unsubstantiated "right to abortion." Writing for the 6-3 majority in Dobbs v. Jackson Women's Health Organization, Justice Samuel Alito stated, "The Constitution makes no reference to abortion, and no such right is implicitly protected by any constitutional provision… It is time to heed the Constitution and return the issue of abortion to the people's elected representatives."

Despite the media's wailing and gnashing of teeth, and despite Democrats' impotent roars of rage, the reality is that the Supreme Court decision was not extreme in any way. It did not reflect the most ardent desires of pro-lifers. It did not, for example, declare a right to life applicable to unborn children under the 14th Amendment's guarantee against the removal of "life, liberty or property, without due process of law." Nor did the decision follow the legally correct advice of Justice Clarence Thomas, who recommended trashing the Supreme Court doctrine of "substantive due process," a persistently and irritatingly vague rubric that generally acts as a pretext for courts to pursue their favored public policy objectives. The decision did not even suggest that the federal Congress had the power to regulate abortion in place of state laws.

No, the Dobbs ruling returns the status of the question of abortion to the status quo ante prior to Roe.

Now states will decide how and when to regulate abortion. Some states, like Texas, will work to bar abortion except in cases in which the mother's life is in danger. Others, like New York, will cheer abortion up until the point of actual birth. No consensus policy is likely to emerge, because there is no consensus on the issue among Americans.

Yet Democrats and the media seem firmly convinced that the re-animation of abortion as a state law issue will somehow translate into 2022 electoral victory. There is little evidence to this effect: State laws generally reflect the opinions of those who live in those states, and the most ardent abortion defenders tend to reside in heavily blue areas where abortion will be freely available. It's hard to believe that Manhattan residents are going to show up to the polls en masse to vote on Alabama's abortion policy—and even if they did, it would make no difference in House or Senate elections in Ohio.

There is another problem for Democrats, too. That problem lies in the simple fact that if Americans *do* vote based on abortion, they don't do so purely based on preferred abortion policy. They do so based on the attitude of the parties toward abortion generally. And today, the party of abortion extremism is the Democratic Party, which long ago abandoned the logically unsound but emotionally appealing rubric of "safe, legal and rare," instead substituting the hideously monstrous "shout your abortion." The Democratic Party moved away from moral condemnation of abortion because Democrats now believe that human happiness is rooted in subjective self-definition, particularly with regard to sexual activity; that biology, particularly pregnancy and childbearing, is an active imposition on such a vision of human happiness; and that abortion is therefore a sacrament to be protected.

Few Americans outside of solid blue areas agree with

these bizarre and ugly notions. So, while Democrats suggest that voters will resonate to their abortion messaging, fearful of abortion restrictions that might prohibit them from terminating their pregnancies, they miss a broader point: their vision of human happiness and the measures necessary to achieve it are not in line with that of most Americans. And that means that the culture war that the Left began is now turning against them, as it should.

Pan(dem)ic

How Bureaucracy Killed Hundreds of Thousands of Americans

January 6, 2021

Over the course of the COVID-19 pandemic, the media have spilled barrels of ink over mistakes by the federal government. We've heard endlessly about the failure to quickly ramp up testing, the confusion over mask-wearing and the debates over proper lockdown policy. But when the history of this time is written, the fundamental mistake made by the United States government won't be rhetorical excesses by the president or conflicting public health advice. It will be the same mistake the government always makes: trusting the bureaucracy.

We now know that the miraculous Moderna vaccine for COVID-19 had been designed by *Jan. 13, 2020*. That was just two days after the sequencing of the virus had been made public. As David Wallace-Wells writes for New York magazine, "the Moderna vaccine design took all of one weekend. ... By the time the first American death was announced a month later, the vaccine had already been manufactured and shipped to the National Institutes of Health for the beginning of its Phase I clinical trial." Meanwhile, for six weeks, Dr. Anthony Fauci assured Americans that there was little to worry about with COVID-19.

Fast-forward to the end of 2020. Hundreds of thousands of Americans have died. Tens of thousands of Americans continue to die every week. The Food and Drug Administration has still not cleared the Oxford-AstraZeneca vaccine, which costs a fraction of the other vaccines (about $4 per dose, as opposed to $15 to $25 per dose for Moderna's vaccine or $20 per dose for the Pfizer-BioNTech vaccine). The FDA approval process cost us critical months, with thousands of Americans dying each day. As Dr. Marty Makary of Johns Hopkins University told me this week, "Safety is their eternal excuse. They are entirely a broken federal bureaucracy... Why did we not have a combined Phase I-Phase II clinical trial for these vaccines?"

This is an excellent question, of course. Phase I trials involve small numbers of participants, who are then monitored. Phase II trials involve larger numbers. Huge numbers of Americans would have volunteered for a combined Phase I-Phase II trial. And even after we knew the vaccines were effective, the FDA delayed. Data was collected by late October that suggested Phase II/III trials had been successful. The FDA quickly requested more results, which it did not receive until November. It then took until Dec. 11 for the FDA to issue emergency use authorization for the Pfizer vaccine. The Moderna vaccine wasn't cleared until Dec. 18, nearly a year after it had first been produced.

The disgrace continues. The government *continues* to hold back secondary doses of the vaccine, despite the fact that the first doses provide a significant effect. As Makary says, "We're in a war. The first dose gives immunity that may be as high as 80 to 90 percent protection, and we can probably give half the dose, as Dr. Moncef Slaoui suggested... We can quadruple our supply overnight."

Meanwhile, states continue to be confused by the Centers for Disease Control and Prevention guidance on how to tranche out the vaccines. It took until nine days after the FDA authorized the Pfizer vaccine for the CDC to release its recommendations. Those recommendations were still complex and confusing and often rife with self-defeating standards—even though it was perfectly obvious from the start that the solution ought to be based on age.

Americans have relied on the government—a government supposedly comprised of well-meaning experts—to get us through a pandemic. The government not only failed with conflicting information and incoherent lockdown policy but also actively obstructed the chief mechanism for ending the pandemic thanks to bureaucratic bloat. If Americans' takeaway from the COVID-19 pandemic is that centralized government is the all-purpose solution, they're taking precisely the lesson most likely to end in mass death in the future.

Lying About 'Misinformation' To Justify Tyranny

July 21, 2021

  This week, President Joe Biden was asked whether he had any message for social media amidst a dramatic rise in the number of diagnosed COVID-19 cases thanks to the delta variant. Biden immediately responded that companies like Facebook were responsible for murder: "They're killing people—I mean, they're really, look, the only pandemic we have is among the unvaccinated. And they're killing people." Meanwhile, Surgeon General Dr. Vivek Murthy said that Facebook had not stopped misinformation thoroughly enough on its platform, calling misinformation a "serious threat to public health."

  None of this is accurate. Facebook is, first of all, a platform; it is not a publication with the same responsibilities of editorial oversight as a publisher. To treat Facebook as such would be to transform its purpose. Furthermore, on a purely factual level, it is simply untrue that Facebook users are disproportionately likely to avoid vaccination—in fact, according to Facebook's statistics, vaccine acceptance in the United States among their users now stands between 80% and 85%, and 3.3 million Americans have used their vaccine finder tool to seek a location for a vaccine.

  So, what's driving the Biden administration's finger pointing? Its broader agenda to utilize the massive market dominance of the social media platforms to squeeze alternative media sources out of existence. Before the rise of social media, most Americans who used the internet for news bookmarked a variety of pages and then visited them individually. Over time, as social media grew and as people began to access stories they liked through an algorithmically controlled newsfeed, Americans used social media for news. This centralized the mechanism for information dissemination.

Now, the left sees an opportunity: If all the news is accessed in one place, by restricting access in that place, the news monopoly once held by legacy media can be reestablished. All that will be required is labeling everyone they don't like "misinformation."

Kara Swisher of The New York Times, who has spent the past several years attempting to pressure Facebook into exactly such censorship, says as much openly. According to Swisher, Biden wasn't wrong to say Facebook was killing people. Actually, writes Swisher, the problem is that Biden restricted his analysis to the coronavirus: "Attempting to stop falsehoods by claiming to offer good information is like using a single sandbag to hold back an impossibly fetid ocean. It's like that when it comes to a range of once-anodyne, now divisive issues, from election integrity to critical race theory to whatever."

"Whatever." Literally any topic on which Swisher disagrees is now dangerous misinformation that must be curbed. This week, NPR went so far as to pressure Facebook to suppress traffic to my website, Daily Wire, on precisely this basis. NPR admitted that we don't print falsehoods, that we don't spread conspiracy theories and that we are honest and open about our conservative perspective. So, why should we be suppressed? Because, according to NPR, we cover "specific stories that bolster the conservative agenda." And, quoting an expert, NPR reports, "If you've stripped enough context away, any piece of truth can become a piece of misinformation."

There it is: even truth can be misinformation. And misinformation kills.

The authoritarianism of the left is in full swing. Americans must spot it and fight it before it destroys our ability to see anything other than that which the left wants us to see.

When Does the COVID-19 Panic End?

August 4, 2021

Two weeks to slow the spread.

That was the original rationale for the lockdowns, masking and social distancing: Prevent transmission of the coronavirus so that Americans could be assured that we would not overwhelm hospital capacity, causing needless death.

Wait until a vaccine is available.

That was the next goal post: an admonition to continue to take precautions to avoid spreading the coronavirus until a vaccine could be developed. Despite the warnings of COVID-19 pessimists that a vaccine would take years to develop, despite the unjustified alarmism of figures like Vice President Kamala Harris that the Trump administration would skew the vaccine protocols to achieve political ends, vaccines were miraculously developed.

Wait until every adult has a chance to get the vaccine.

That was the final rationale for caution. And as states began to tranche out vaccines by the millions, every person above the age of 12 in the United States was given the opportunity to get vaccinated. As of today, over 90% of adults over the age of 65—the most at-risk population in the United States—have been vaccinated, and more than 70% of all Americans over age 18 have been vaccinated as well.

And yet.

We are told that we are experiencing a massive COVID-19 crisis. We have been told that the vaccinated must mask up again; that the unvaccinated should be barred from public establishments; that children must be masked in school. We have been told that America faces doom and death on a daily basis and that we're seeing a crisis akin to the last wave of the coronavirus in January. We're masking up and checking vaccine cards in Washington, D.C., in San Francisco, in Los Angeles, in New York.

The statistics simply do not bear this out. According to the seven-day rolling average as calculated by The New York Times, fewer than 400 Americans per day are dying of COVID-19; at the height of the pandemic, well over 3,000 were. In Washington, D.C. (total population: 692,000), that number is 0; in San Francisco County (total population: 875,000), that number is 0; in Los Angeles County (total population: 10 million), that number is 9; in New York City (total population: 8.4 million), that number is 3.

The current delta variant spike has resulted in a massive case count, particularly in Florida, but deaths are not following cases—and if the United States follows the pattern of the United Kingdom and the Netherlands, we're likely to see the case count begin to crater in the next few weeks. Those who are vaccinated are not dying of COVID-19; their death rate is minuscule. Those who are unvaccinated have *chosen* not to vaccinate; they are independent adults capable of determining their own approach to risk and reward.

All of which requires us to ask the question: When are we done?

When are we done telling children to mask up to protect adults who don't want to vaccinate? When are we done telling businesses to close up or bar customers based on vaccination status? When are we done with mask mandates (data suggests that mask mandates are ineffective, even if masking is sometimes useful), with evidence-free social distancing rules (six feet is pure conjecture), with the ever-vacillating, Delphic pronouncements of Dr. Anthony Fauci?

We have hit the goal posts; every adult now has the capacity to protect himself. There are no other realistic goal posts: Zero COVID-19 cases was never a realistic goal.

When is the job of government done?

And yet.

Our public health "experts" continue to promote more and more outrageous restrictions. This week, National Institutes of Health Director Francis Collins went so far as to recommend that vaccinated parents mask up in their *own homes* around their *own children*. There is no limiting principle to this, no end goal. There is only a bureaucratic and political elite unwilling to treat citizens as adults, recognize their own limitations and leave us all the hell alone.

And if we accept that, we deserve nothing less than subjection to their paternalistic control.

Welcome to the Forever Pandemic

August 25, 2021

This week, as President Joe Biden attempted desperately to distract from his ongoing surrender in Afghanistan and the attendant chaos in its wake, the White House turned its eyes once again to the issue of COVID-19. On Monday, Biden pressed private industry to mandate vaccination, stating, "Do what I did last month, require your employees to get vaccinated or face strict requirements." Meanwhile, the ubiquitous Dr. Anthony Fauci told CNN's Anderson Cooper, "I respect people's freedom, but when you're talking about a public health crisis… the time has come, enough is enough. We've just got to get people vaccinated."

Meanwhile, the Biden administration also pressed private sector vaccine mandates. Fauci announced on MSNBC that everyone should mask, vaccinated or unvaccinated: "Instead of worrying what kind of mask, just wear a mask. Wear a surgical mask, a cloth mask… We need to wear masks." Biden went further, extending his push for masks to small children: "You have the tools to keep your child safer… make sure that your child is masked when they leave home."

Put aside the fact that the data support none of these policy prescriptions: There is little evidence that vaccine mandates will push the unvaccinated into overcoming their hesitancy; vaccine mandates are likely to press the unvaccinated into common spaces in which they are *more likely* to transmit the virus to other unvaccinated people, who are in far more danger than the vaccinated; the delta variant, according to former Obama advisor Dr. Michael Osterholm, makes a mockery of cloth masks; according to the University of Waterloo, surgical masks are essentially ineffective against delta; there is literally *zero* data demonstrating that masking children in schools has been effective in reducing transmission of the coronavirus; and children are at exorbitantly low risk from the virus, given that according to the Centers for Disease Control and Prevention, just 361 Americans under age 18 have died of COVID-19 during the entirety of the pandemic.

Instead, focus on a simple fact: our pandemic is now officially endless.

At the beginning of the pandemic, we were told to accept lockdown measures in order to prevent our hospitals from being overwhelmed—to flatten the curve. We did so. Then we were told to mask up to prevent transmission of the virus while we developed a vaccine. We did so. Then we were told to wait to unmask and gather in large numbers until after every adult had the opportunity to be vaccinated. We did so.

Now, every adult in America—every person over age 12—has had the ability to get vaccinated. Well over 75% of all Americans aged over 65 have been double-vaccinated. A majority of people in the United States have been double-vaccinated. And yet we are still told that mask mandates are necessary—presumably to prevent those who have already had the opportunity to be vaccinated from contracting COVID-19, since the vaccinated are at extremely low risk of hospitalization and death even if a breakthrough infection occurs.

How can this be justified?

On simple logical grounds, it can't. The government has now done all it can to provide protection to those who want it; those who demand government restrictions have provided no metric for success by which proposed restrictions end and we all go back to normal life. Is it deaths? Obviously not: Hawaii has an indoor mask mandate for everyone, despite a seven-day rolling average of two deaths per day and a population of 1.4 million. Is it hospitalizations? No: Australia is in a state of complete lockdown, despite a grand total of 119 people in the ICU in a country of 25 million people and with baseline ICU bed capacity of at least 2,378. Is it infections? We have no standard by which infectivity level is low enough to go back to normal: Schoolkids are being told to mask despite no evidence that children are at serious risk or are a main vector of transmission.

Which means that zero COVID-19 has become the goal.

And that's not a goal, that's a pipe dream.

But that pipe dream means we are stuck in pandemic mindset permanently. There is literally no goal post. Which means that Americans have a choice: either we can choose to live under restrictions forever to prevent a minute risk of post-vaccination hospitalization and death, or we can go back to normal. If we choose to give up our freedom for the chimera that government can end risk entirely, we deserve none of the freedoms we supposedly cherish.

An 'Abundance of Caution' Mentality Leads to Tyranny

December 1, 2021

This week, governments around the globe spun into full-scale panic thanks to the revelation of the so-called omicron variant of COVID-19. As of this writing, we know that omicron is likely more transmissible than prior variants. We have no evidence, however, that omicron is more deadly. To the contrary, Dr. Angelique Coetzee, chairwoman of the South African Medical Association, explained that the symptoms associated with omicron were "mild," explaining, "we don't see severely ill patients."

Were that true, that would make omicron a cause for optimism. That's because delta is already highly infectious and herd immunity seems to be a pipe dream—which means that if someone has the choice between an omicron infection and a delta infection, one would wish for the omicron infection. If omicron was to crowd out a deadlier variant, that would be a positive development for global health.

Yet the reaction from our institutional leaders has been completely unhinged. We have been told by the director of the Centers for Disease Control and Prevention that every American above the age of 18 ought to get a booster shot of the COVID-19 vaccine, despite scant evidence that boosters lower the hospitalization and death rates from COVID-19 for the young (they certainly do for those over age 60). Dr. Anthony Fauci has emerged to nod gravely at the possibility of vaccine mandates for air travel and new mask mandates. Gov. Kathy Hochul of New York announced a state of emergency allowing for the suspension of elective surgeries.

The predictable result: markets have plunged. They've plunged not because of omicron itself, but because the private sector knows that the public sector may hammer away at economic freedom again. Our political class has failed throughout the pandemic; perhaps their only real success was in assigning a grab bag of cash for pharmaceutical companies that developed vaccines. Other than that, nearly all public policy measures have been ineffective.

The same will hold true of omicron. Omicron is already present in nations around the world. Lockdown policies were ineffective in curbing the pandemic outside of isolated countries around the globe; the return of lockdown won't be any more successful. Mask mandates have been markedly disassociated from actual disease replication rates. And vaccines are already widely available; those who are afraid of omicron will get vaccinated, and those who aren't won't.

Now would be a good time to take a breath.

And yet our public officials are pathologically incapable of humility. This time, they suggest, will be different; this time, they'll prevent disease from spreading. It seems that the most powerful in our society have a vested interest in the lie that they can stop disease, death and privation. They won't let go of that lie, lest citizens see through the veil and seize back power over their own lives.

Instead, we're told that we must hand over *more* control to our authoritarian-minded leaders, to the self-appointed Scientific Experts (TM)—all out of an "abundance of caution," of course. Strangely, that abundance of caution never seems to extend to unprecedented interventions in everyday life or the global economy. In those areas, our elites throw caution to the wind.

A true "abundance of caution" mentality would suggest that before we destroy our institutions again—before we overthrow free markets in the name of welfarism, checks and balances in the name of health authoritarianism, and individual liberty in the name of safety—we see some data. Otherwise, heavy-handed "solutions" will always be the measure of first resort, long before we even know whether a crisis has materialized.

The Big Government COVID-19 Lie

December 22, 2021

On Oct. 30, 2020, just days before the presidential election, Joe Biden tweeted, "I'm not going to shut down the country. I'm not going to shut down the economy. I'm going to shut down the virus."

This was a lie.

It was a lie because *nobody can shut down the virus.*

Government does not have the power to end disease, as a general matter. When it comes to a wildly transmissible coronavirus specifically, no government can end the virus. Even the sainted Dr. Anthony Fauci has admitted as much: "we're never going to eradicate this... elimination may be too aspirational."

Which means that government should not aim for elimination; it can aim for some level of control. That control must be balanced with countervailing concerns, ranging from suppression of economic freedom to the effects of social isolation. This means that the lowest-cost intervention was incentivization and distribution of vaccines—a service performed by the Trump administration. The worst form of control would be overbroad, coercive restrictions that fail to achieve their objectives.

And yet it is precisely those forms of control now being sought by Democratic mayors and governors, as well as the Biden administration. To make such tactics even more puzzling, Democrats are pursuing such restrictions in the face of an extraordinarily transmissible variant—some 70 times more transmissible than delta—that has far lower death rates than prior variants.

Such restrictions include vaccination passports,

mask mandates, mass testing, and vaccination mandates. Vaccination passports will not control the spread of omicron, because the vaccinated are capable of spreading COVID-19. Mask mandates will not stop the spread of omicron; nothing short of N95 masks would do much to even slow that spread, even theoretically. In practice, mask mandates have not achieved their desired effect, as omicron spikes in places like New York City demonstrate. Mass testing will not control the spread of omicron, because asymptomatic people will not test—and if we quarantine millions of asymptomatic and mildly symptomatic people, we will shut down the economy and our school system. And vaccination mandates will simply result in supply chain shortages, including within our health care system, as well as ugly social divisions.

So, why pursue useless—no, counterproductive—COVID-19 restrictions?

Because the big-government lie must be maintained. It is an article of faith. And faith requires reason-free sacrifice—it requires skin in the game, demonstration of devotion. To pursue rational policy would evidence no fealty to the notion of government-as-protective-god. To pursue irrational policy and then demand obeisance—this is the mark of the faithful. And if you are not faithful, you are a heretic.

And so regulatory genuflection becomes a test of virtue. Effectuating strict regulations is a sign of moral strength, of belief in the myth of government as catholicon. Pushing back against those restrictions is a sign of heresy.

On Oct. 22, 2020, in a debate with President Donald Trump, Biden said that "anyone who is responsible for not taking control… anyone who is responsible for that many deaths should not remain as president of the United States of America." This was incorrect. The truth is that anyone who claimed that he *could* take control of a virus should be held responsible for the consequences of that lie.

But that will only happen when Americans abandon the cultic worship of government and return to reality. And Biden and Democrats will fight such blasphemy with every weapon in their arsenal.

The Year of Living Unreasonably

December 29, 2021

In 2020, Americans learned that if emergency dictated, we could lock down, mask up, and blow out spending to temporarily stymie the impact of a global pandemic. We learned that if uncertainty required massive response, we could mobilize massive response, including the creation of new vaccines within one year.

And in 2021, Americans learned that it's easier to flip the switch on toward top-down control and government dependency than to turn it back off.

We have vaccines that likely reduce the chances of hospitalization and death from COVID-19 (somewhere between 0.05% and 0.1%) to below the infection fatality rates of the flu (somewhere between 0.1% and 0.2%). We have effective therapeutics, including a new therapeutic pill that will reduce post-COVID-19 diagnosis hospitalization and death by around 90%.

And we have a new strain of COVID-19. Omicron reportedly infects at 140 times the initial rate of COVID-19, and about 70 times the rate of delta; it hospitalizes, according to South African data, at about 20% the rate of delta. Which means that nearly everyone will get omicron, and that very few people will die.

And yet here we are, nearly two years into the COVID-19 pandemic, with our expert class informing us that we must vaccinate and boost, no matter our age (in reality, only those who are older than 65 or immunocompromised truly require a booster); that we must continue to mask up, even if that means using cloth masks against omicron (even Leana Wen, CNN's resident COVID-19 hawk, calls cloth masks "facial decorations");

that we must vaccinate and mask our small children and possibly shut down schools again (children are at near-zero statistical risk from COVID-19); that we must test the asymptomatic, sending the economy into soft lockdown (attempting to prevent transmission is a fool's errand given the transmissibility of omicron); that we must put in place vaccine passports (even though the vaccinated are getting and transmitting omicron); that we must continue to spend money at record rates in order to prop up an economy that we are destroying for no good reason.

We have, in other words, lost our minds.

It turns out that learned helplessness sets in extraordinarily quickly—and that proponents of such learned helplessness become unreasonably angry when others refuse to engage in it. Thus, President Joe Biden spent most of this year deriding his political opponents as friends to the virus and attempting to mobilize sentiment against the unvaccinated. Today, the media continue to preach that red states are the COVID-19 problem despite the fact that case counts are at record highs in states ranging from New York to New Jersey to Massachusetts.

Biden did announce this week that there was "no federal solution," stating that the pandemic would be "solved at the state level." This came after Biden tried to cram down a federal vaccine mandate, chided former President Donald Trump for his supposed failures of leadership, and went to rhetorical battle with Florida Gov. Ron DeSantis for refusing to engage in COVID-19 hysteria.

But his administration just as quickly bought back Biden's comments, suggesting that "we're going to get through this by working together"; meanwhile, the sainted Dr. Anthony Fauci announced the possibility of a vaccination passport for air travel.

It may take the election of 2022 to remind blue-state

Democrats and the elitists in our media that unreasonable policy has consequences. Either way, we can only hope that 2022 is the year that Americans return to reality rather than continue living in a pandemic-paranoid fantasy.

The COVID-19 Impact of Expressive Individualism

January 26, 2022

Philosopher Robert Bellah once posited that modern Western human beings identify themselves in a peculiar way: as emotional cores, surrounded by baser material. According to Bellah, we are expressive individualists—meaning that "each person has a unique core of feeling and intuition that should unfold or be expressed if individuality is to be realized." This mode of self-definition wars with older, more traditional modes, which suggest that our identities lie in how we interact with the world and society around us. Expressive individualism, by contrast, suggests that we are not truly ourselves unless the world confirms all of our feelings and intuitions. As professor Carl Trueman points out, this viewpoint is essentially solipsistic; he explains, "When identity is psychologized, and the pursuit of happiness becomes a subjective, psychological matter, anything that challenges that paradigm is deemed damaging and oppressive."

We see this phenomenon most obviously in the bizarre insistence by transgender advocates that not only are they men trapped in women's bodies or vice versa, but that society mirror that incorrect self-perception. But expressive individualism also manifests in other contexts, such as belief in racial essentialism, denial of parental rights, and objection to science itself.

It even crops up in reference to COVID-19.

COVID-19 should be a paradigmatic example of where expressive individualism fails: It is an exogenous shock to the individual, a reality that exists no matter the subjective thoughts or feelings. The data map out individuals' risk factors; particular actions, like vaccination, can lower the risk of hospitalization or death for most people, no matter the intuitions of individuals who object. All of which mean that we should be able to track that data, and to change our response to the pandemic based on new data.

And yet we have now, as a society, psychologized even COVID-19 in expressive individualist terms. Thus, after Bari Weiss pointed out on Bill Maher's show that the public health establishment has failed time and again to follow the data, that the vast majority of those who have been vaccinated are safe from COVID-19, and that we ought to consider life returning to normal, a massive backlash ensued—backlash from those least vulnerable to COVID-19, who have now internalized a sense of COVID-19 moral superiority. Thus, Sara Haines of "The View" lamented, "I think some of the things we've learned in this pandemic will stay the same. I may never ride the subway without a mask, I may never go indoors to big crowds and feel comfortable without a mask." Michelle Goldberg of The New York Times explained, "What you can't do is force other people, whose vulnerabilities might be much greater than your own, to agree with your risk assessments and join you in moving on while the pandemic still rages."

But that's precisely what Goldberg and Haines are doing—forcing other people to take measures that the science does not support in order to maintain *their* emotional comfort. Boosters are not stopping omicron. Nothing short of N95 masks is stopping omicron. The disease is now endemic, which is why Dr. Hans Kluge of the World Health Organization's European region stated this week, "Omicron offers plausible hope for stabilization and normalization."

But there will be no normalization for those who have made pandemic paranoia a feature of their identity. That's because the public health establishment has now successfully cultivated a large group of people who measure their moral value by just how compliant and panicked they remain over COVID-19: Fully 68% of people fully vaccinated with boosters remain very or somewhat worried about getting sick from COVID-19 in the next year, compared with just 39% of those who are unvaccinated. This is the precise opposite of what the public health authorities should have achieved—but expressive individualism has won the day once again, conflating one's feelings with one's identity group.

Canada Goes Tyrannical

February 16, 2022

This week, Canadian Prime Minister Justin Trudeau, the lightweight, unpopular elected leader of a country with a 93% vaccination rate for those over 60 and a total vaccination rate of 84%, announced that he would invoke the Emergencies Act in order to crack down on the Freedom Convoy—a group of protesters opposed to government vaccination mandates for truckers. Trudeau breathily announced that invocation of the law was in fact "reasonable and proportionate." His public safety minister, Marco Mendicino, said that the actions were required thanks to "intimidation, harassment, and expressions of hate."

Why the government would need to invoke emergency powers in order to move some trucks remains beyond understanding; after all, the police had just removed trucks from the Ambassador Bridge, reopening that trade artery with the United States. Meanwhile, provinces across Canada have already begun alleviating their COVID-19 restrictions, from vaccine passports to masking. There is no emergency here that would justify use of the Emergencies Act—as even the BBC noted, "It is so far unclear which scenario Mr. Trudeau would rely on to justify the use of the Emergency Act—(the relevant threats have not) been clearly present in Ontario."

Nonetheless, Finance Minister Chrystia Freeland explained that the government would be extending laws designed to stop terror funding to now encompass crackdowns on political dissent: "Financial service providers will be able to immediately freeze or suspend an account without a court order. In doing so, they will be protected against civil liability for actions taken in good faith." In plain language, this means that the government of Canada has now empowered banks to freeze accounts who give money to political causes the government doesn't like.

The move to de-bank disfavored political actors has already been gaining steam—in January 2021, PayPal blocked a Christian crowdfunding site from using its services; the next month, Paypal announced it would work with the Left-wing Southern Poverty Law Center to find users to boot. As one of Paypal's original creators, David Sacks, wrote, "when your name lands on a No-Buy List created by a consortium of private fintech companies, to whom can you appeal?" In Canada, it's worse than that: The de-banking has become government sponsored.

And if Trudeau is able to invoke emergency powers to de-bank his political opponents—people he has labeled racists simply for opposing his vaccine mandates—where, precisely, does this end? What's to stop powerful political actors from violating liberties on the same pretext?

The answer, of course, is nothing. And perhaps that's the point: from now on, dissent against Left-wing perspectives may be criminalized. Watch what you say—your bank account is on the line.

Over the course of the past century, the political Left made a promise: that if they were granted more and more centralized power, they would protect their citizens, particularly during times of emergency. That promise was always a lie, but the pandemic exploded that lie in particularly egregious fashion. This left the Left with two options: to abandon that article of faith, an idea central to their entire worldview; or to persecute heretics. Trudeau, unsurprisingly, has chosen the latter. Emergency powers will be necessary until the people enthusiastically agree that their betters in government ought to rule them.

The COVID-19 Authoritarians Panic over the End of the Mask Mandates

April 20, 2022

This week, a federal judge in Florida finally struck down a federal mask mandate from the Centers for Disease Control and Prevention. An extensive number of executive branch agencies have acted in an authoritarian manner throughout the COVID-19 era: The Occupational Safety and Health Administration infamously attempted to cram down a vaccine mandate on every private employer in America, a policy struck down by the Supreme Court; the CDC blocked evictions for over a year based on the premise that millions would be thrown from their homes if they didn't take action. But the CDC's travel mask mandate has been particularly annoying for Americans, given the fact that all over the country, Americans have either been vaccinated or acquired natural immunity, and there is no evidence whatsoever that cloth or surgical masks do anything against the omicron variant of COVID-19.

Nonetheless, the CDC pressed forward this month with a new extension to its mask mandate, despite the fact that the CDC simultaneously argued that beginning in late May, it would relieve Title 42, a regulation designed to allow Border Patrol to turn away likely illegal immigrants at the border. That regulation was rooted in the premise that a COVID-19 emergency negated the legal requirement to process asylum seekers. The White House provided zero justification for the CDC's extension; instead, White House press secretary Jen Psaki struggled to explain why toddlers on planes should remain masked, but attendees at the White House press room didn't have to. "I'm not a doctor," she spat.

Of course, Psaki's lack of medical background hasn't prevented her from announcing that the best standard of medical care requires minors who are gender confused to receive puberty blockers on the path toward genital-mutilating surgery. But Americans shouldn't expect consistency from their moral betters in the White House.

Upon the announcement of the judge's ruling striking down the CDC mask mandate on the grounds that the CDC hadn't actually bothered to follow its own regulatory procedures, the Left went into spasms of apoplexy. Public figures began posting pictures of themselves donning masks on planes: former Obama senior adviser Valerie Jarrett tweeted, "Wearing my mask no matter what non-scientists tell me I can do"; Roland Martin tweeted, "I don't give a damn what some grossly unqualified Donald Trump judge said. I'm double masked and wearing goggles on this Nashville to DC flight. I had COVID in December. Y'all can KISS MY ASS about me not wanting it again. And any fool saying they don't matter is a damn liar."

Now, it should be said that nobody has actively *banned anyone from wearing a mask*. It is your choice to don one, as epidemiologically useless as such a gesture may be. But those on the Left seem to be under the wild misimpression that anything not prohibited is now mandatory—an act of pure intellectual projection springing from the Left's insistence on collective rulemaking. For those on the Left, individual freedom represents a threat to everyone; to allow individuals the ability to choose therefore undermines the entire scheme. Those on the Left simply project this mindset onto everyone else. Thus, they believe that anyone who opposes mask mandates wants to force everyone to unmask.

This is untenable but predictable: for those on the Left, the collective is the irreducible unit of politics. There are no individuals. And anyone who disagrees is, in the words of Robin Givhan of The Washington Post, "childish and selfish."

Or perhaps—just perhaps—the most childish and selfish among us are those who beg government agencies to exceed their statutory authority in order to ensure that we all mirror their favored priorities. Perhaps those who have spent two years declaring their authority over every aspect of Americans' lives ought to consider the possibility that we're happy to let them ruin their own, but that we would prefer they leave us alone. And most of all, perhaps the COVID-19 paranoiacs ought to spend just a moment considering whether there is a space between mandatory and prohibited where others might be granted a smidgen of liberty.

Newspeakonomics

How Blue City Governance Is Destroying Blue Cities

June 16, 2021

 This week, a video from a San Francisco Walgreens went viral on Twitter. The video depicted a man standing next to his bicycle, loading up a garbage bag with products. The man then rides his bicycle down the aisle, past a security guard, who limply throws out a hand to try to grab the bag; the shoplifter simply brushes past him, then rides out the door.

 This sort of thing has become exceedingly common in San Francisco. In late May, Thomas Fuller wrote in The New York Times, "At a board of supervisors hearing last week, representatives from Walgreens said that thefts at its stores in San Francisco were four times the chain's national average, and that it had closed 17 stores, largely because the scale of thefts had made business untenable." Employees at Walgreens had been told to stand aside as shoplifting took place because security officers had been assaulted repeatedly.

 All of this is the result of a 2014 California ballot measure that reclassified nonviolent theft as a misdemeanor, so long as the thief took less than $950 worth of material. Thieves quickly hit on a strategy: Hit up different stores for less than $950 worth of stuff. Then, amid the Black Lives Matter protests and riots of 2020, San Francisco decided to crack down on the police. Mayor London Breed announced that booking photos would no longer be released, lest the prevalence of Black and brown faces lead to stereotyping; she announced a $120 million cut to the police and sheriff's department over the next two years, in the interest of "prioritizing investments in the African American community"; in the first six months of 2020, 23 officers resigned from the force.

Property crime has skyrocketed. It's not just shoplifting: burglaries increased nearly 50% year-on-year in 2020, and car theft jumped 34%. Meanwhile, the streets are littered with garbage, and have been for years thanks to lax law enforcement. In 2018, a survey of 153 blocks in downtown San Francisco showed trash on every block, 41 blocks "dotted with needles" and 96 blocks with open human feces.

This form of governance has become all too common. Los Angeles, my former hometown, has steadily declined in terms of livability. Suburban areas have been inundated with homeless vagrants, often openly shooting up, while the police have been directed to do nothing; Venice Beach has become an enormous open-air homeless encampment. Seattle has morphed from the Emerald City into a refuge for those living on the street, regardless of the risks to other citizens.

There is a reason why Americans are fleeing America's major cities. The problem predated COVID-19, and it will post-date it, too. Americans like having a Walgreens in their neighborhoods. They enjoy being able to walk down the sidewalk without severely mentally ill homeless people—who should be in institutions where they can receive actual care—urinating on curbs. They should not have to instruct their children to hop over used needles on street corners.

Yet the governance of "compassion" continues. So does the migration away from such foolhardy policy. The top outbound states in America, according to North American Moving Services, were all deep blue: Illinois, New York, California, New Jersey and Maryland. The top inbound states were all red or purple: Idaho, Arizona, South Carolina, Tennessee and North Carolina.

At some point, there will be no more Walgreens in San Francisco. Then we will undoubtedly hear about how this is the product of systemic racism and white privilege; we will hear tell of the brutality of American capitalism. The truth is far simpler: Where Leftist governance reigns, criminality thrives. And where criminality thrives, Americans flee.

Our Empathetic Authoritarians

July 28, 2021

America has a crisis of empathy.

That crisis isn't expressed as lack of charitable giving: Americans give approximately seven times what Europeans do to charity per capita. And it isn't expressed as an unwillingness to spend on a governmental level: The United States currently spends more money than any nation in the history of the world.

The crisis of empathy isn't even about an inability to walk in other people's shoes: America is one of the most racially and religiously tolerant nations on earth.

The American crisis of empathy rests in a simple fact: America is now divided over two mutually exclusive definitions of empathy. That divide is unbridgeable, and it's tearing the country down the middle.

One group of Americans—call them Neutrality-Driven Empaths—defines empathy as treating people as individuals capable of free choice and deserving of equality under the law. In this view, empathy manifests in respect for the capacity of other human beings, and in understanding that they make different decisions than you would. This version of empathy doesn't require that we agree with anyone's decisions, but that we understand that it is not our job, absent significant externalities, to rule them.

The other group of Americans—call them Emotion-Centered Empaths—believes that empathy means mirroring solidarity with subjective feelings in policy. In this view, empathy means expressing agreement with someone else's specific feelings, refusing to assess whether those feelings are merited or justified and then shaping policy around assuaging those feelings.

Neutrality-Driven Empaths believe that politics ought to be about solutions geared toward equality of individuals before the law. Policy and emotional empathy may come into conflict in this view. Emotion-Centered Empaths believe the opposite: They believe that politics ought to be about emotional solidarity rather than finding solutions. Policy must follow emotional empathy in this view.

To take a rather stark example, consider the question of black student test performance. Neutrality-Driven Empaths will suggest that meritocratic standards are in fact the only neutral rules that can be applied to education, and that such standards have acted as a ladder for a wide variety of human beings of various races; that if a disproportionate number of black students underperform on such tests, that may merit empathy, but it doesn't merit discarding the standards. Emotion-Centered Empaths will, in direct opposition, suggest that the mere fact of black student underperformance *requires* discarding testing regimes—to do otherwise would be to abandon solidarity with those who underperform, to ignore the myriad factors that undoubtedly led to the underperformance in the first place.

The battle between Neutrality-Driven Empaths and Emotion-Driven Empaths creates a massive political asymmetry. That's because Neutrality-Driven Empaths acknowledge that while people may disagree over policy, that does not mean they are uncaring or cruel. But for Emotion-Driven Empaths, the opposite is again true: If policy is directly correlated with empathy, failure to agree represents emotional brutality and cruelty. Not only that: There can be no agreeing to disagree, because to suggest that people bear consequences for their actions is in and of itself uncaring and unempathetic. It lacks solidarity.

The empathy gap is a crisis. If you believe that empathy means treating people as individuals capable of reasoning and acting under neutral rules, we can have a society. If you believe that empathy means shaping policy around solidarity with subjective feelings, rules become kaleidoscopic, variable and fluid—and compulsion is generally necessary in order to effectuate such rules.

Empathy for people as full human beings means recognizing their agency, understanding their differences and holding fast to equality before the law. If we reject those principles in favor of a high-handed and paternalistic approach to power politics, freedom will not survive.

When Politicians Call For 'Fairness,' They're Usually Lying

September 22, 2021

This week, President Joe Biden attempted to inject life into his ailing presidency by dragging out of the closet the hoariest of political cliches: "fairness" in taxation. Touting his new $3.5 trillion tax and spending bill, which would radically increase corporate taxes, personal income taxes and so-called sin taxes, Biden stated, "It's not enough just to build back; we have to build back better than before... I'm not out to punish anyone. I'm a capitalist. If you can make a million or a billion dollars, that's great. God bless you. All I'm asking is you pay your fair share. Pay your fair share just like middle-class folks do."

Of course, those who earn high incomes don't pay like middle-class folks do. They pay far, far more. IRS statistics show that the top 1% of income earners pay more in federal income tax than the bottom 90% combined—while the top 1% earned 21% of all income in 2018, they paid 40 % of all income tax revenue. The top 10% paid over 70% of all federal income tax. In fact, according to the American Enterprise Institute, those in the highest quintile of income earners pay, on average, well over $50,000 per year in net taxes—taxes minus government benefits received—while those in the bottom 60% of income earners *receive* net tax benefits. According to The Washington Post, the top 10 % of American income earners pay nearly half of all income taxes, compared with just 27% for the top 10% of Swedes, 31% for the top 10% of Germans, and 28% for France's top 10%.

So what, precisely, does Biden mean by "pay their fair

share"?

Perhaps he means simple sloganeering. Like Rep. Alexandria Ocasio-Cortez donning a Cinderella ball gown emblazoned with the words "TAX THE RICH" to the Met Gala—a dress made by Aurora James, a woman who owes tens of thousands of dollars in back taxes and who has received over $40,000 in federal pandemic aid—class warfare sloganeering is more about the sloganeering than the class warfare. No Democrat seems prepared to define what "fairness" constitutes, other than "a word I use to pander to the rubes, while hobnobbing with the rich."

And Biden's "fairness" pitch has to do with good economic policy, of course. In 2008, then-Sen. Barack Obama was asked during a debate about raising the capital gains tax, even if it lowered net government revenue. He answered, "I would look at raising the capital gains tax for purposes of fairness." In other words, Obama explicitly stated that he would *damage the economy* on behalf of a vague, kindergarten notion of equal outcome.

In the end, the "tax the rich to be fair" notion rests on a simple lie: the lie that income distribution is purely a matter of privilege or luck. It isn't. In the main, in a free market system, income distribution is the result of successful decision-making that must be incentivized rather than punished if we wish to see a more prosperous society. Some people game the system; some are indeed beneficiaries of insider deal-making. But most success in capitalism is due to innovation, entrepreneurialism and creativity. Biden's "fairness" cuts directly against these core elements of progress on behalf of political pandering.

If we truly care about fairness—a more nuanced and complete definition of fairness that encompasses rewards for productive decisions and disincentives for counterproductive decision-making—we must abandon the politically convenient notion that those who earn more have somehow stolen from the system and must be punished for their crimes. Lack of distributive equality does not equal unfairness, and anyone who argues differently abandons the real world—and the possibility of a better life for everyone—in favor of the flattering lie that all roads ought to end in the same basic material outcome.

No, Government Spending Isn't 'Zero Cost'

September 29, 2021

This week, President Joe Biden made the incredible statement—sycophantically repeated by the press—that his $3.5 trillion budget bill, which includes major spending initiatives on everything from climate change to Medicare, would be "free." Biden tweeted, "My Build Back Better Agenda costs zero dollars. Instead of wasting money on tax breaks, loopholes, and tax evasion for big corporations and the wealthy, we can make a once-in-a-generation investment in working America."

This asinine notion immediately rocketed around the political sphere. White House press secretary Jen Psaki explained, "The reconciliation package will cost zero dollars." Rep. Pramila Jayapal, D-Wash., said, "This is a zero-dollar bill because it's all going to be paid for with taxes on the wealthiest corporations and the wealthiest individuals, which makes it more popular than it even was before." Members of the media began repeating the line ad nauseum. The reason was obvious: Democrats are trying to cudgel Republicans into acquiescing.

Putting aside the contention that Biden's bill would be paid for through tax increases—a doubtful proposition, given that the Democrats have been playing accounting games by extending particular allowances for just a handful of years, or backloading new costs until years down the road—the baseline notion that government spending is zero-cost so long as it doesn't take on new debt is bonkers. It's the equivalent of arguing that so long as someone pays for a cocaine-fueled gambling binge in Vegas in cash, the experience has been cost-free.

Biden, however, goes even further. In his addled brain, allowing taxpayers to retain their own money is "wasting money"; spending trillions of dollars on social programs that pervert market incentives and often achieve the precise opposite of their stated intentions is an "investment." Such a designation divests language of meaning. If you steal my wallet and find $100 inside, proceed to inform me that giving me back $20 would be "wasting money," snidely notify me that you will be "investing" in a steak dinner for yourself and then cap your performance by stating that the dinner is "zero-cost," you would deserve a rather thorough thrashing. Do it in the context of national politics, however, and the media will cheer.

All of this is predicated on a lie: that the state is the ultimate source of property and wealth. If that were true, the state would certainly have every ability to maximize its own power by shifting that property around to political allies. In fact, this is precisely what Thomas Hobbes argued in "Leviathan": that the sovereign was the ultimate arbiter of property, as the ultimate repository of force.

The American system was founded in direct opposition to this idea. As James Madison wrote, "Government is instituted to protect property of every sort... This being the end of government, that alone is a just government, which impartially secures to every man, whatever is his own." Madison added, "That is not a just government, nor is property secure under it, where the property which a man has in his personal safety and personal liberty, is violated by arbitrary seizures of one class of citizens for the service of the rest."

Biden would call just such sorts of arbitrary seizures "investments." After all, they're free. To Biden, such language seems natural: he is a career-long ward of the state, on the taxpayer dole every year of his life since the age of 29—the only exceptions being the years between his vice presidency and his presidency, when he was giving speeches and writing books about his government years while allegedly avoiding half a million dollars in taxes. To him, taxpayer dollars *are* free, and they *have been* an investment: in him. Now, he simply wishes to extend that logic outward, using taxpayer dollars to "invest" in his legacy, in structures that incentivize dependency and therefore Democratic electoral power.

What's the harm? It's cost-free.

Except it isn't. The engine of American growth has never been the government. It has been restrictions on governmental power and bureaucratic arbitrariness. Innovation requires freedom; investment requires both liberty of choice and impartiality of governing system. The heavy hand of government will be damnedly costly.

The Nation in the Bubble

October 13, 2021

This week, the Biden administration received just the latest slap in the face from cruel reality: An economic report showing just 194,000 jobs added in the month of September, short of the 500,000 jobs forecast by most economists. The unemployment rate dived to 4.8% from 5.2%—not as a result of job gains, but as a result of more and more Americans dumping out of the work force. Meanwhile, inflation continued to pick up steam, with domestic labor shortages exacerbating supply-chain bottlenecks.

How should we explain the bizarre spectacle of a nation that should be booming stagnating instead?

For the Biden team, the answers range from the completely idiotic (lack of government stimulus, after the greatest single spending binge in world history) to the merely foolish (the delta variant, caseload from which has taken a nosedive). The actual answer, however, is simple: We have spent a year training Americans to believe that work is alternately unsafe, unavailable or unnecessary.

First, we have trained vaccinated Americans to believe that they are unsafe. According to a CBS News poll in July, just 48% of those who were unvaccinated said they were worried about infection from the delta variant, compared with 72% of fully vaccinated Americans—this despite the fact that vaccinated Americans are rarely hospitalized and nearly never die from COVID-19. Yet Biden himself continues to trot out the lie that the vaccinated are not safe from the unvaccinated: In early September, he pushed for a national workplace vaccine mandate, claiming that it was necessary in order to "protect vaccinated workers from unvaccinated co-workers." But that's precisely what the vaccine was for. It's no surprise, then, that so many vaccinated people—the first people who should be eager to reenter workplaces—are instead hesitant to go back to the office.

Second, we have barred the unvaccinated from going back to work. Biden suggested that vaccine mandates would heighten employment by making the vaccinated feel safe. But that obviously hasn't worked: Instead, all he's done is take jobs from those who were always willing to go back to work. Thousands of Americans have been laid off thanks to vaccine mandates, including in crucial industries like health care and air travel.

Most importantly, we have trained Americans to believe that work is unnecessary. As jobs go unfilled, a certain contingent of politicians celebrates—they say that workers have been unchained from their jobs, and that this is a net positive. In August 2020, Rep. Alexandria Ocasio-Cortez, D-N.Y., told Vice, "Only in America, when the president tweets about liberation, does he mean 'go back to work'... I think a lot of people should just say no. We're not going back to work." Paying people to stay home, in this view, is merely incentivizing businesses to pay more for fewer hours, thus making life better for those who choose to work; for everyone else, the government dole.

Now, most Americans have rejected this last lesson. Most Americans want to work; most Americans are in fact working. Hence the unpopularity of the Biden administration spending plans, which most Americans feel artificially suppress economic growth and stifle opportunity. But Biden and Democrats are counting on the long-term play: grow government, breed dependence and ultimately shift the relationship between Americans and the government.

Biden promised he wouldn't shut down the economy or the country—he'd shut down the virus. Instead, thanks to his progressive priorities, he's made the pandemic a problem with no logical endpoint in sight, shutting down the economy and the country in the process—all in pursuit of his transformational vision. The current labor shortage is a feature of the plan, not a bug. But Biden didn't promise transformation in the 2020 race—he promised a return to normalcy. And so, his approval ratings are cratering. As they ought to.

The End of Risk and the End of Civilization

October 20, 2021

Human beings aren't great at assessing risk.

In 1979, psychologists Daniel Kahneman and Amos Tversky posited a new branch of behavioral economics, which they titled prospect theory. One of their key findings was that human beings are naturally loss-averse—we generally are willing to forego the probability of gains in order to minimize the chance of losses. Because of our loss aversion, human beings are also subject to what Kahneman and Tversky label the "planning fallacy": our self-serving bias toward believing that we are capable of planning for contingency more successfully than we are. As Kahneman writes, "Exaggerated optimism protects individuals and organizations from the paralyzing effects of loss aversion; loss aversion protects them from the follies of overconfident optimism." If we feel that we can solve problems, we might be more likely to take risks—and if we feel that risks are a problem, we might be more cautious with our plans.

But what if the problem we are seeking to solve is *risk itself?* What if our policymakers aren't concerned with counterbalancing loss aversion on behalf of more productive risk-taking? What if, instead, our policymakers lie to us, and tell us that risk is no longer necessary *at all?*

This is the situation in which we currently find ourselves. As a society, we have become so addicted to the elimination of risk that we are willing to believe any politician who provides us a purported roadmap. A large percentage of the country believes in nearly religious fashion that all risk can be mitigated, so long as we grant the authorities and experts absolute power. We have been told that we need no longer face health risks, so long as we give the government power to mandate vaccines, mask our children and lock down our businesses—even without solid evidence that such measures are effective. We have been told that we ought to delegate all of our economic policymaking to unelected centralized bureaucracies, which serve as the source of both our monetary and fiscal policy, and that this will insulate us against the possibility of financial difficulty. We have been told that individually planning for the future, which entails risk—delayed gratification is always a risk—should be foregone in favor of a cradle-to-grave government safety net.

To mitigate risks to myself, the easiest measure is to create an authority that controls everyone. Risk itself is the enemy: someone else might undertake risks, and those risks might have indirect effects that harm me. Better to live in the warm embrace of control by experts than in the chaotic world of individual decision-makers.

This is the road to authoritarianism.

A healthy civilization *requires* risk-taking. Innovators are risk-takers. Disincentivizing that risk destroys innovation. Working is risk-taking. Disincentivizing that risk destroys work. Building for the future is risk-taking. Disincentivizing that risk destroys responsibility. The fundamental good of liberty lies in the incentivization of risk. As F.A. Hayek put it, "If there were omniscient men, if we could know not only all that affects the attainment of our present wishes but also our future wants and desires, there would be little case for liberty." But, Hayek points out, we are not omniscient; we do not know who will provide progress, or how. Progress requires risk; liberty ensures the ability to take risk.

We thus have a choice before us between the false promise of individual enervation and endless paternalistic caretaking from centralized authority and the real and chaotic world of liberty and risk. Which option we choose will decide whether our civilization survives.

Punishing Achievement Is Punishing Everyone

October 27, 2021

This week, Democrats settled on an area of apparent commonality: the desire to eat the rich. According to Treasury Secretary Janet Yellen, "Senator Wyden and the Senate Finance Committee... would impose a tax on unrealized gains on liquid assets held by extremely wealthy individuals, billionaires." While Yellen refused to call this a "wealth tax," House Speaker Nancy Pelosi had no such qualms: "We probably will have a wealth tax," she said.

This has long been a talking point for the most Marxist-leaning Democrats, like Sen. Elizabeth Warren, who famously proposed a 2% wealth tax on all assets of a family above $50 million and 6% on all assets above $1 billion. Elated Warren supporter Adam Jentleson told The Washington Post, "Biden's agenda was about to fall apart, but Warren had a plan for that."

So, what do wealth taxes do? They destroy value by taxing unrealized value. Say, for example, that you are a business owner who created a company now valuated at $1 billion. And say that you have built that business over the course of the last five years, paying yourself a post-tax, post-expenditure salary of $5 million per year. You would be liquid to the tune of $25 million. Under Warren's proposal, $950 million of those unrealized assets would be taxed at 2%, meaning that you would be on the hook for an annual tax of $19 million. You would have no choice but to liquidate your stock, undermining its price and endangering the growth of your company.

Wealth taxes have been tried in a variety of

countries, and they have regularly failed. When France created a wealth tax, some 42,000 millionaires left; French President Emmanuel Macron eventually killed it. From 1990 onward, nine out of the 12 European countries that had a wealth tax followed Macron's lead and killed their wealth taxes.

So, what's the point of a wealth tax if, in the end, it will fail?

The point is the punishment. Biden and Warren are seeking to tax dollars that *do not yet exist,* because the people who have created those dollars are worthy of sanction. While Biden constantly blathers that he is a capitalist who doesn't seek to punish earners—only to make them pay their fair share—he's simply lying. Earners in America certainly pay their fair share: the top 1% of income earners pay approximately 40% of all income taxes while earning just 21% of all income; the highest quintile of income earners pay virtually all net taxes in America after income transfers by the government. This isn't about a "fair share." It's about disincentivizing wealth creation, demonizing it, treating it as a mark of sin.

Unfortunately, we have mainstreamed such economic and moral idiocy. When we speak of the wealthy as the "privileged," we betray our own unwillingness to speak the obvious: High-income earners provide more and better goods and services to people than lower-income earners. That is why their income is high. Income is a reflection of consensual transactions resulting in voluntary trades. Innovation and risk-taking *must be rewarded* in order for them to take place; to then attribute success to "privilege" or "luck" is to pretend that a free-market system is some sort of lottery. It isn't. If we decide that it is somehow more altruistic and moral to receive government benefits than to take risks that result in economic success, we destroy the economic mechanism that has generated all of our prosperity—and the individuals who make that mechanism work.

And that's the point. What begins as a small tax on an upper crust doesn't stay that way. The original income tax contemplated in the United States was 1% applied to the lowest tax bracket, and 7% on those making $500,000 or more. Today, the top marginal income tax rate is 37%; income above $86,000 is taxed at 24%. Eventually, the agenda becomes clear: going after all earners, not merely those at the top. When achievement is punished, there are no income barriers.

The So-Called Meritocracy Isn't The Problem

November 10, 2021

In 1958, British sociologist Michael Young coined the term "meritocracy" in his satirical novel, called "The Rise of the Meritocracy." Its point was simple: When intelligence and effort are selected by any society as the basis for success or failure, those with such merit begin to comprise their own class. That class hardens into an elite that brooks no dissent and stratifies society. As Young would say in 2001, "It is good sense to appoint individual people to jobs on their merit. It is the opposite when those who are judged to have merit of a particular kind harden into a new social class without room in it for others."

This general point has become the basis for illiberal thinkers, both on the Left and on the Right. Philosopher Michael Sandel, in his latest book, "The Tyranny of Merit: What's Become of the Common Good?" argues that the very notion of a meritocracy carries with it an unescapable and unsustainably selfish moral judgment. According to Sandel, "The ideal itself is flawed. Meritocracy has a dark side. And the dark side is that meritocracy is corrosive of the common good. It encourages the successful to believe that their success is their own doing and that they therefore deserve the bounty that the market heaps upon them… it generates hubris among the winners. They believe that their success is their own doing and they also believe, implicitly at least, that those who struggle must deserve their fate as well."

This argument can be marshalled on behalf of both Right-wing and Left-wing critiques of the current capitalist order. On the Right, the argument is that capitalism—

rewarding, as it generally does, intelligence and hard work—undermines important social institutions. David Brooks argues in The New York Times that meritocracy destroys "civic consciousness, a sense that we live life embedded in community and nation, that we owe a debt to community and nation and that the essence of the admirable life is community before self." On the Left, the argument is that meritocracy justifies existing imbalances of economic and social power.

The debate over meritocracy, however, depends on a crucial failure to distinguish between economic merit and moral merit. The term meritocracy itself does a great disservice in smudging this distinction—that is, in fact, why Young coined the term that way. Instead of linking "merit," with all of its moral implications, with intelligence and hard work, we ought to instead use the term "skillsocracy." Any economic system that rewards skills produces positive externalities. A person who works hard, who innovates—who creates better products and services and trades those products and services with someone else—enriches not only those involved in the voluntary trade, but also the society at large by raising the bar on the products and services that will eventually become available to everyone. Every innovation is quickly followed by competition, by the spread of that innovation to a broader and broader market—which is why peasants today in Western societies live better than kings did centuries ago.

By contrast, any economic system that prizes an alternative set of values has *negative externalities*. Should we adjudicate economic distribution by race? Creed? Religion? Simple ethical preference? Disincentivize risk-taking, guarantee incomes by "moral occupation," and watch as misallocation of labor destroys economic progress entirely; watch as society breaks down as those who produce less for their fellow man are rewarded more.

This does not mean that those who are most dexterous should "run society." To create such a system would, in fact, undermine the skillsocracy itself, since it would allow the centralized will of some to undermine the innovative efforts of all. Economic mobility must remain predicated on skill, or the skillsocracy is undermined.

This also does not mean that the skillsocracy actually acts as a measure of moral good. Intelligence is largely inborn, and thus not a moral attribute per se; propensity for hard work may be partially genetic but can be cultivated. But in a moral society, we find noneconomic ways of treasuring virtue. We cultivate friendships; we provide honor and respect; we build communities on virtue and exclude those people who do not abide by such moral standards.

This means that a skillsocracy ought not be at odds with a virtuous society. Far from it. The so-called "meritocracy" need not devolve into a *moral* measure of intelligence and hard work; indeed, in a healthy society, it must not. But by the same token, we must never destroy the skillsocracy as a supposedly expedient way to revive moral living. That effort would be both unsuccessful and wildly counterproductive.

The Death of California

December 15, 2021

In "The Hunchback of Notre Dame," Victor Hugo told the tale of Esmerelda, a gypsy dancer falsely accused of attempted murder, set to be hanged by an unjust state. Quasimodo, the titular hunchback, swings down from the cathedral of Notre Dame and saves her, carrying her off while crying "Sanctuary!" In fact, throughout European history, churches provided places of safe haven for accused criminals; the claim of "sanctuary" is made to this day by people seeking refuge from the law.

It is strange, however, to see the language of sanctuary adopted to protect precisely the sort of activity abhorred by anyone of religious bent: abortion. The secular sacrament of abortion has become so sacred, however, that the governor of California, Gavin Newsom, recently announced his intent to make his state the first abortion sanctuary in the nation. "We'll be a sanctuary," Newsom announced. "We are looking at ways to support that inevitability and looking at ways to expand our protections."

The state of California, according to Newsom's Democratic legislative allies, could provide travel expenses including gas, lodging, transportation and child care for those seeking to kill their unborn children. Already, some 15% of America's abortions occur in California, according to the Guttmacher Institute. That number would skyrocket if the state began subsidizing abortions across the land.

None of this is particularly surprising. It is telling, however, that as California sinks into the mire, it embraces ever more radical social policy. This is a state that currently houses—no pun intended—some 162,000 homeless people, a number that increased approximately 24% from 2018 to 2020. About a quarter of all homeless people in the United States currently reside in California.

Meanwhile, crime in California has become endemic, with smash-and-grabs roiling major cities and even wealthy residents murdered in their homes. This week, the head of the Los Angeles police union, Jamie McBride, warned people to stay out of the city, explaining, "We can't guarantee your safety. It is really, really out of control." Even former LA Mayor Antonio Villaraigosa laments, "Rome is burning."

And California's economy trails the nation's, too. According to the Bureau of Labor Statistics, California is tied for the worst unemployment rate in the nation, at 7.3%. And while California is currently experiencing a seven-day rolling average of just 67 COVID-19 deaths—compared with 550 at the height of the pandemic—Newsom recently reimposed another monthlong statewide indoor mask mandate.

So why does California keep embracing ever-more-radical policy? Because the radicalism is itself the moral justification for policy failure. Sure, Democrats can argue, crime and homelessness are out of control, the economy is stagnating, and businesses are leaving. But that's morally excusable, because California seeks a higher purpose: the purpose of Leftist utopianism. Thus, Newsom has little to say about California's stagnation, but much to say about how California will push new laws targeting gun ownership.

For years, Democrats have claimed that California leads the nation. We can only hope they're wrong.

The Great Re-Sorting Is Here

January 12, 2022

This week, the incoming New York City Mayor Eric Adams—the supposed rational corrective to uber-radical outgoing Mayor Bill de Blasio—announced that he would allow legislation to proceed allowing local voting for 800,000 noncitizens. The same week, the legislature in California took up a bill that would establish single-payer health care in the state, paying for the increase in costs by essentially doubling taxes.

Americans have been fleeing the most liberal states in mass numbers. Those numbers are about to increase even more.

Between July 2020 and July 2021, approximately 352,198 residents of New York State embarked for warmer climes. Over that same period, the District of Columbia lost 2.9% of its population. California lost 367,299 people via net domestic migration. Illinois, another failing blue state, saw a net domestic out-migration of 122,460 people.

Where did all these blue state refugees go? To red states, of course. Texas picked up 170,307 Americans migrating from other areas. Florida picked up 220,890 people. Arizona picked up 93,026. Idaho had the fastest annual population increase in the nation.

The only region of the country to gain population was the South, which now holds 38.3% of the total population of the country—and which picked up 657,682 Americans migrating from different areas. The Northeast is now the least populous region in the United States, and saw a net population decrease of 365,795 residents. All net increase in population in the West was due to births and international migration, not domestic moves.

It's not just individuals—it's companies. Facebook's parent company, Meta, just signed the largest-ever lease in downtown Austin for floors 34 through 66 of the tallest tower in the city. Elon Musk has relocated his company headquarters to Texas. My own Daily Wire relocated in 2020 from California to Nashville, Tennessee.

In other words, red state governance is a magnet; blue state governance is a disaster. Yet blue states cannot change course. They cannot simply jettison their adherence to failed ideas like single-payer health care or voting for illegal immigrants. To do so would be to acknowledge error. And so instead, they are banking on unearned moral superiority—virtue signaling—to fill the gap where good governance should be. Thus, red states are grandma-killing hellholes (where blue state legislators vacation); red states are brutal suppressors of voting rights (where Stacey Abrams wants to run for governor again); red states are filled with vicious dog-eat-dog trickle-down capitalists (who must be taxed to pay for national spending programs).

None of this is bound to convince Americans to vote Democrat. It's not designed to do so. Democrats have banked on a consistent electoral strategy since former President Barack Obama's 2012 victory—the strategy of driving out a base comprised of minority voters and college-educated women. But that strategy is collapsing—as Ruy Texiera, once the nation's leading proponent of that strategy, admitted in November, "if Hispanic voting trends continue to move steadily against the Democrats, the pro-Democratic effect of nonwhite population growth will be blunted, if not cancelled out entirely, and that very influential Democratic theory of the case falls apart."

It's falling apart in real time. But Democrats can't pull out of the tailspin. They're too invested in the lie that their programs are popular to notice how many Americans are calling up U-Haul.

The Quest to Destroy Work

January 19, 2022

This week, after spending time vacationing in the disease-ridden hellscape known as Florida, Rep. Alexandria Ocasio-Cortez, D-N.Y., came down with COVID-19. It was a tragic blow to the irrepressible Instagram star, who was forced to quarantine. But then, like an extraordinarily inaniloquent phoenix rising from the ashes of the dread omicron variant, she returned to her web audience with a message for the ages.

"Welp, so it happened," she wrote, in truly Tolstoyan fashion. "Got COVID, probably omicron. As of today I am thankfully recovered and wrapping up quarantine, but COVID was no joke. For a while I've noted the term 'mild' is misleading when the bar is hospitalization and death." After dispensing with the preliminary medical advice, Ocasio-Cortez got down to business—or rather, to the business of avoiding doing business. She explained, "The idea of forcing people to work just 5 days after symptoms start is sociopathic and 100% informed by a culture that accepts sacrificing human lives for profit margins as a fair trade."

Now, this is, to put it mildly, dumb as a box of rocks. No one is suggesting that people with significant COVID-19 symptoms ought to go back to work. And nobody is sacrificing human lives by encouraging those with waning or no symptoms to return to the office. Businesses cannot run without employees.

Fortunately for us, the brilliant, "So Fresh, So Face" congresswoman has a solution: community. And by community, she means government. And by government, she means your money. "If you've noticed," she writes, "much of the emphasis on media conversations on COVID are individualistic—if there's one lesson I think we as a country are repeating until we learn, it's that community and collective good is our best shot through our greatest challenges—way more than discorded acts of 'rugged individualism' and the bootstrap propaganda we've been spoon-fed since birth... In a world of MEs, let's build team WE. (Blue heart emoji)"

So, what exactly is the illustrious congresswoman proposing? Presumably, that businesses pay people to stay home if they are mildly symptomatic or asymptomatic; or that the government regulate businesses into such activity; or that taxpayers pay the freight. This accords with other proposals from Ocasio-Cortez, such as her Green New Deal idea to provide "economic security to all those who are unable or unwilling to work."

And Ocasio-Cortez's message is mirrored by even higher-level politicians like Speaker of the House Nancy Pelosi, who once proposed that Americans be provided nationalized health care so that they could leave their jobs en masse, thereby freeing them to "be a photographer or a writer or a musician, whatever, an artist." In the view of the far Left, work is a bad, foisted upon unwilling individuals by a cruel and arbitrary system. If only the system could be run properly, in top-down fashion by great minds like Ocasio-Cortez or Pelosi, Americans would be freed from the tyranny of everyday life.

Of course, precisely the opposite is true. Someone, as it turns out, has to pay the bills. And what's more, Americans generally *like* working. They find work fulfilling. Depression rates are twice as high among the unemployed than the employed—and more than three times as high for those unemployed for more than 27 weeks. Most Americans aren't eager to spend their days locked in their apartments waiting for government checks. And they're even less eager to spend more money at the store thanks to supply issues caused by lack of production due to labor shortages.

But Ocasio-Cortez and Pelosi don't have to worry about all of that. Ocasio-Cortez can always Instagram Live from her apartment or Zoom into congressional conference calls. And she never has to worry about the profit margins she spends so much time deriding; she can undercut those for others at her leisure.

Democrats used to pose as the party of labor. Now, they're increasingly the party of those who wish to avoid it at all costs.

It's Time for the Market Pushback to Begin

March 23, 2022

This week, The Walt Disney Company, which has approximately 200,000 employees spanning the globe, decided to radically reshape its politics in response to a tiny contingent of radical activists. According to The Wall Street Journal, Disney CEO Bob Chapek had steadfastly refused to embroil his company in the politics of the various states and countries where Disney did business; he correctly noted that the job of the company was to continue to make magic, not to do the political bidding of any favored coterie.

Then, the state of Florida passed a law that would ban the indoctrination of small children into left-wing perspectives regarding gender identity and sexual orientation. And all hell broke loose. Senior Disney executives began circulating letters stating that the company opposed the Florida legislation, which opponents had falsely labeled the "Don't Say Gay" bill (the bill doesn't mention the word gay once). And some employees threatened a walkout if Disney did not reorient itself toward their favored political position.

So Chapek caved. He sent a letter to staff stating, "You needed me to be a stronger ally in the fight for equal rights and I let you down. I am sorry." He then pledged a listening tour, the formation of a task force to cater to LGBT priorities, and opposition to a Texas measure that would prosecute genital mutilation or hormonal sterilization of children. The company also committed itself to injecting its radical left-wing values in content, including "new content for children and family" infused with those values.

According to reports, Disney even went so far as to commit to including a lesbian kiss in its upcoming children's film "Lightyear."

Chapek is caving because this is what left-leaning corporations do: they listen to their most outraged left-wing contingent, and then parrot them. Instead of giving an answer proper to an employer besieged by employees threatening a walkout—telling the employees to get back to work or join the unemployment lines—major companies simply surrender. Meanwhile, parents who simply wish their children to be entertained without being indoctrinated watch in perplexed horror as radical activists design content for their children.

In order to combat this nonsense, those who oppose the hijacking of major companies by the Left must get organized—and they must create alternatives. That's what we've tried to do at The Daily Wire. In 2021, Harry's Razors withdrew their advertising on one of our shows, citing a "values misalignment." What precisely was the problem? Our host had stated that men are men and women are women, and that sex is immutable.

So, we fought back. This week, we launched Jeremy's Razors, a razor company dedicated to the proposition that everyone, regardless of politics, deserves a good shave. We are here to provide you excellent products for you to use. And we will never slap our customers in the face thanks to the priorities of a woke few. That's why our motto is simple: "Shut up and shave."

If corporations decide to go woke, there must be competitors who assure that they will go broke. And we hope to fill that gap. We only hope others will follow our lead.

Yes, It's Biden's Inflation

April 13, 2022

This week, America received news of yet another shocking inflation report: over the past 12 months, inflation has skyrocketed 8.5%, outpacing wage gains by 2.9%. That inflation has flooded every area of American life, from gas (up 48%) to airfare (24%) to furniture (16%) to milk (13%). Inflation is costing the average American family hundreds of dollars per month—and, as we know, inflation is a highly regressive tax, harming those at the bottom of the income spectrum the most.

For its part, the Biden administration blames Russian President Vladimir Putin's invasion of Ukraine. White House press secretary and incipient MSNBC employee Jen Psaki announced, "we expect March CPI headline inflation to be extraordinarily elevated due to Putin's price hike," and blamed gas prices alone for the spike. That, of course, is ludicrous. In February 2021, the month after Biden took office, the inflation rate was just 1.7%. In April 2021 it spiked to 4.2%. By May 2021, the inflation rate was 5%; it remained in that range until October 2021, when it spiked to 6.2%; it then spiked again to 6.8% in November 2021 and 7.5% in January 2022.

In other words, the problem ain't Putin.

It also isn't supply chain issues alone. The core inflation rate in Europe has remained well below that of the United States; the harmonized index of consumer prices (HICP) was 5.9% in February 2022 in the Europe area, compared with 7.9% in the United States.

So, what *is* the problem? The problem lies in loose monetary policy from the Federal Reserve for years on end, combined with wildly irresponsible economic policy from the Biden administration. Begin with the Federal Reserve. Between 2008 and 2015, the Federal Funds Effective Rate was essentially zero. It rose to 2.39% in May 2019, then dove back down to zero amidst the COVID-19 recession. This means that the Federal Reserve essentially subsidized borrowing and spending for years on end.

But the problem didn't stop there. During the COVID-19 downturn, the Federal Reserve purchased some $4 trillion in assets, injecting liquidity into the economy in the mistaken belief that the problem was lack of demand, not lack of supply. This superheated the economy; as supply chains attenuated, prices rose dramatically.

All of this was accompanied by ridiculously spendthrift policy from the Biden administration. The Trump administration, along with a bipartisan contingent in Congress, spent nearly endless amounts of money as the American economy was subjected to an artificial coma. But the Biden administration entered office with a working vaccine and COVID-19 on the wane—and then proceeded to inject trillions more in spending into the economy. In 2020, the government spent approximately $6.6 trillion in federal outlays; in 2021, the year of recovery, the government spent $7.2 trillion.

That spending was wildly unjustifiable. With vaccines available and people going back to work, the Biden administration had a responsibility to leave the economy alone. Instead, Biden insisted on reshaping the economy according to his whim. As Ezra Klein lamented to former Treasury Secretary Larry Summers, "there was a reason the Biden administration wanted to run the economy hot… it felt, finally, like we were reaching people on the margins. We were putting a lot of firepower to do that… And then for that to turn into this horrifying inflation problem, which is now eating back those wage increases… I recognize the world doesn't have to please me, but it is maddening."

Yes, reality is maddening. But not quite as maddening as the predictable results of ignoring financial reality, then lying about it in order to blame someone else.

The Elitists Who Want to Rule the World

May 25, 2022

  Klaus Schwab is the head of the World Economic Forum; he founded the organization in 1971. Each year, the WEF hosts a massive conference in Davos, Switzerland, with thousands of world leaders, diplomats and experts on various topics gathering to trade ideas about how best to cooperatively run the world. Lest this characterization be seen as overstating the case, Schwab himself said as much this year in opening the conference: "The future is not just happening. The future is built by us, by a powerful community as you here in this room. We have the means to improve the state of the world. But two conditions are necessary. The first one is that we act all as stakeholders of larger communities, that we serve not only self-interest but we serve the community. That's what we call stakeholder responsibility. And second, that we collaborate."

  This is the call to action for elitists the world over. They appoint themselves the representatives of global interests—without elections, without accountability—and then create mechanisms of national and international order to control citizens over whom they claim to preside. Schwab himself has decoded his favorite term, "stakeholder capitalism." He wrote in Time magazine in October 2020, "Free markets, trade and competition create so much wealth that in theory they could make everyone better off if there was the will to do so." To do so, however, would require taking hints from Greta Thunberg, #MeToo and Black Lives Matter; it would require "building... a virtuous economic system" in which companies abandon their core mission of serving customers and shareholders and instead embrace answering questions like "What is the gender pay gap in company X? How many people of diverse backgrounds were hired and promoted? What progress has the company made toward reducing its greenhouse-gas emissions?"

All of this extraordinary arrogance is predicated on a perverse view of how successful change works within decentralized systems. As Schwab himself acknowledges, free markets have generated more prosperity than any system in human history. But that's because free markets are *not* a top-down imposition, a system created by conspiratorial muckety-mucks in a back room somewhere. Free markets were the outgrowth of centuries of evolutionary societal progress: gradual recognition that private ownership was the greatest incentive toward work and innovation; incremental understanding that individual rights are the only alternative to endless conflict; step-by-step acceptance that decentralized sources of knowledge are both broader and deeper than centralized ones. The most powerful and durable institutions we have are traditional because, as F.A. Hayek wrote, they are "a product of cumulative growth without ever having been designed by any one mind."

For Schwab and his ilk, however, it's precisely such an evolutionary approach that must be ended. Instead, he and his rationalist buddies—brilliant businessmen and ambitious politicians, striving bureaucrats and myopic experts—will cure the world of its ills, so long as we grant them power. Or, more likely, so long as they seize power in the name of "stakeholders" to whom they are never answerable.

One of the great ironies of the past several years is the gap between the elitists' perception of themselves. To the elitists, their solutions failed because citizens of the world lacked the will to listen to them; to the citizens, the elitists failed because their prescriptions were ill-founded. Yet so long as the elitists retain their power, they will continue to push forward their utopian dreams at the expense of those they purport to serve.

Joe Biden's Economy Is a Disaster

June 15, 2022

This week, the stock market took a turn into bear territory on the heels of yet another brutal monthly inflation report. With the Federal Reserve considering larger rate hikes in order to tamp down record inflation, the possibility of a near-term recession now looms quite large, despite the feeble protestations of Treasury Secretary Janet Yellen. As former Clinton Treasury Secretary Larry Summers—the man who predicted President Joe Biden's inflation—stated, "I think when inflation is as high as it is right now, and unemployment is as low as it is right now, it's almost always been followed, within two years, by recession."

All of this was perfectly predictable. Firehosing money into an already-hot economy was a recipe for inflation—and yet that was precisely the policy pursued by the Federal Reserve and the Biden White House. According to The Wall Street Journal, the Biden White House and the Fed thought that the post-COVID-19 period would follow the 2007-2009 pattern: "weak demand, slow growth, long periods of high unemployment and too-low inflation." This was incontestably preposterous. The 2020 economic crash was not the result of systemic flaws in the economy like the 2007-2009 subprime mortgage crisis; it was the result instead of an artificially induced economic coma, supported by an unprecedented infusion of government cash, preceded by a historic economic boom.

This meant that when vaccines became available, when Americans headed back to work, when children went back to school, we should have been poised for an explosion in demand. To instead predict weak demand, and to build an extraordinary framework of continuing fiscal and economic stimulus on that basis, was an act of either total insanity, epic stupidity or purposeful malice. Perhaps it was a combination of all three. As the Journal observed, "many Democrats saw their control of the White House and Congress as a rare opportunity to shift Washington's priorities away from tax cuts favored by Republicans and toward expensive new social programs." Or, as Biden himself put it this week, "I don't want to hear any more of these lies about reckless spending. We're changing people's lives!"

They sure are. It turns out that "experts" in the back room constructing a supposedly better world rarely consider the possibility of unpredicted side effects. They are so busy building glass castles in their minds that they neglect the realities of human behavior. The result is generally that those the "experts" seek most to help are actually those harmed the most.

But the Biden White House refuses to change course. Instead, they insist that the American people are too foolish to understand just how good they have it; that the answer is more government spending; that the Federal Reserve, whose loose monetary policy prompted the current price spiral, will magically draw the proper balance between rising interest rates and low unemployment.

The real answer to America's current economic woes is simple, and the same as it ever was: Leave Americans alone. Stop pumping money. Stop subsidizing boondoggle projects directed at bolstering political allies. And stop pretending that our supposed intellectual superiors have the ability to predict, control and boost an economy comprised of 330 million citizens, all of whom are better qualified to make decisions for themselves than an incompetent and incoherent president and his unjustifiably arrogant lackeys.

The World Stage

This Is Not Normal

January 27, 2021

For four years, we were informed by our establishment media that President Donald Trump's behavior was "not normal." The abnormality of Trump's behavior became a near rallying cry for the self-appointed heroes of journalism, who spent every waking hour poring over his bizarre tweets and his bloviating self-absorption. The media dedicated themselves to preventing Trump's supposed normalization.

Now, the media inform us, we have been graced by the most normal normal person to have ever normalled: President Joe Biden. Biden, they proclaim, is utterly boring, nondescript, barely worthy of coverage. His administration, too, is paradigmatically normal. Yascha Mounk of The Atlantic tweets, "It is so nice to have a boring President." Alleged media watchdog Brian Stelter asked this week whether Biden is "making the news boring again," adding, "The Biden White House is clearly a break from the chaos and incompetence of Trump world."

For his part, Biden obviously revels in this sort of coverage. This week, his favorite ice cream flavor (chocolate chip) was tweeted out as well as a retweet of first lady Jill Biden's announcement that Champ and Major, the new first pets, had entered the White House.

On a personal level, Biden is clearly more "normal" than Trump—although treating Biden, a career politician worth nearly $10 million, as the height of normality is rather stunning. The goal for the establishment media isn't to point out merely that Biden is a sort of American Everyman. It's to use that supposed normalcy to disguise the fact that his agenda is absolutely *abnormal*.

The dirty little secret of the Trump administration is that despite Trump's personal abnormality, his agenda was well in line with past precedent, and with mainstream American opinions on everything from taxes to military policy. Trump did not radically shift American policy. Biden will. Within the first five days of his presidency, he issued 30 executive orders, compared with four for Trump, five for Barack Obama and zero for George W. Bush. Those executive orders included endorsement of radical reinterpretation of American history; killing the Keystone XL pipeline, along with its attendant estimated 11,000 American jobs; forcing the military to allow troops to undergo gender reassignment surgery; and forcing federally funded institutions to allow biological men who identify as transgender to compete alongside biological women, among others. He is reportedly pursuing an immigration plan directed toward reopening America's borders. He has staffed his Cabinet by intersectional box-checking.

Biden's policy is indeed radical. But because Biden is presented as a normal person, we're supposed to ignore all of that. We're supposed to simply be grateful for the "return to normalcy"—complete with caving to the teachers unions that seek to keep schools closed indeterminately, reentering a long-dead deal with the Iranian theocracy, firing government staffers with whom he disagrees and lying openly about the vaccine distribution plan he inherited.

Meanwhile, our media pat themselves on the back. It's rare to see a profession declare itself irrelevant, but that's what many in the media are doing these days. According to Stelter, it's "refreshing" that Biden's team promises accountability and transparency. According to Margaret Sullivan of The Washington Post, the media must learn their lesson from the Trump era and cover Democrats *more* sycophantically.

Joe Biden may be a relatively normal guy. But none of this is normal. And pretending it is represents just another way for the media to reject legitimate criticisms of an administration seeking radicalism right off the bat.

Biden Sets Everything on Fire

May 12, 2021

Joe Biden is the luckiest man to ever assume the presidency.

He succeeded an unpopular figure. He was inaugurated just two weeks after the dramatic storming of the U.S. Capitol by extremist Donald Trump supporters seeking to stop the certification of the 2020 election, which was also the beginning of the year after widespread race riots. He inherited COVID-19 vaccines and a vaccine rollout plan, and could rightly expect to ride the tsunami of natural economic recovery that was predicted for the aftermath of the COVID-19 pandemic; he inherited a series of historic Middle Eastern peace deals.

In other words, President Biden had it easy. All he had to do was *nothing*. He could expect a new era of good feelings emerging from a tumultuous time. He could expect a booming economy, a more peaceful Middle East, a solution to the pandemic. All he had to do was calm the waters.

This, after all, was what Americans voted for: not a transformational figure or a figure of radical change but a stodgy, supposedly empathetic grandfather figure who could barely be bothered to leave his basement for the entirety of the presidential campaign. Normalcy could be restored by installing a nearly inanimate object as president.

Instead, Biden has served as a facade for the most radical administration in modern American history. And America is already paying the price.

In his first few months in office, Biden rammed through a $1.9 trillion spending package that completely rewrote the bargain between individuals and the state, shifting the incentive structure for people to go back to work. He simultaneously proposed another $4 trillion in spending—to go along with the annual $4 trillion budget. The result: skyrocketing inflation in commodities, along with dramatic labor shortages resulting in an April shortfall of three-quarters of a million new jobs.

Simultaneously, he downplayed the efficacy of a vaccine he insisted was the key to ending the pandemic. His Food and Drug Administration pressed pause on a highly successful vaccine based on six cases of blood clots; his Centers for Disease Control and Prevention rewrote its school reopening guidelines, apparently with input from the teachers unions. He wore a mask publicly despite being vaccinated, despite being outdoors, despite being indoors with others who had been vaccinated—and declared such activity "patriotic." The result: widespread vaccine hesitancy and a tremendously uneven national reopening, with red states going back to normal and blue states continuing nonsensical shutdowns.

He ramped up the rhetoric with regard to racial polarization, injecting the terms "anti-racist" and "equity" into every element of federal policy, supplanting meritocracy and individual rights with equality of outcome and outright discrimination. The result: undercutting police forces nationally, resulting in a continuing crime wave in America's biggest cities.

And he abandoned the Trump administration's Middle East policy, refunding the Palestinians with money that will obviously go to terrorist groups and defy the Taylor Force Act; making concessions to the Iranian terror regime; and pressuring Israel. The result: riots in Jerusalem, chaos on the Temple Mount and an increase in regional Iranian aggression.

We're only four months into Biden's presidency. He's going for broke: He wants his legacy, and if that legacy comes at the cost of the economy, the polis and international stability, so be it. If the conflagration we've seen thus far is any indicator, Biden won't leave a lot standing when he's done.

If You Side With Hamas, Your Anti-Semitism Is Showing

May 19, 2021

For the past two weeks, rockets have been fired into civilian areas of Israel by the terrorist group Hamas. Hamas' charter openly calls for the destruction of the state of Israel, which would entail an anti-Semitic genocide; its 1988 charter explicitly and openly calls for such a genocide. Hamas spends tens of millions of dollars in foreign aid not on helping the citizens of the Gaza Strip but on building terror tunnels and rocket capacity to strike at the Jews. Hamas fires its rockets from civilian areas, seeking to force Israel to kill Palestinian civilians so Hamas can propagandize about supposed Israeli human rights atrocities. Hamas locates its military facilities inside hospitals, journalist headquarters, schools and mosques. Hamas aims its rockets indiscriminately at civilians in Israel, killing Jews, Arabs and foreign workers.

Israel, meanwhile, routinely calls building supervisors in Gaza to warn them to evacuate buildings before bombing them. One such conversation, broadcast by Sky News, went like this:

Israeli military: "Listen, we are going to bomb the building."

Palestinian building supervisor: "You want to bomb? Bomb whatever you want."

"No, brother, we need to do everything we can so you don't die."

"We want to die."

"But you have a responsibility for children's lives."

"If the children need to die, then they'll die."

"God forbid. God forbid. What do you want to die?"

"This is how we reveal your cruelty."

The media coverage of the conflict has been predictably morally absurd. The Associated Press, an outfit that has regularly covered up Hamas' atrocities, has condemned Israel for hitting a Hamas building in which the AP had offices. Trevor Noah suggested that Israel's military superiority means that Israel must absorb hundreds of rockets per day and allow its civilian population to live under the shadow of radical Islamic terrorism. "If you are in a fight where the other person cannot beat you, how hard should you retaliate when they try to hurt you?" he asked. HBO's John Oliver accused Israel of "killing civilians and children."

Members of the Democratic Party's radical, anti-Semitic fashion have been no less morally inverted. Rep. Rashida Tlaib has encouraged President Joe Biden to cut off Israel's defense supplies. Rep. Ilhan Omar has accused Israel of "terrorism." Rep. Alexandria Ocasio-Cortez has called Israel an "apartheid state," despite the fact that Arabs are full citizens of Israel while not a single Jew lives under the predations of Hamas. And this week, nearly 200 Democrats voted not to cut off funding to groups linked with Hamas.

The conflict between Hamas and Israel is not a dispute over borders: Israel withdrew from the Gaza Strip a decade and a half ago. It is not a dispute over religion: Israel allows Muslims full freedom of worship throughout Israel, *particularly* on the Temple Mount, Judaism's holiest site, where Jewish worship remains essentially forbidden in favor of kowtowing to Islamist diktats. It is not a dispute over homes in Sheikh Jarrah, a suburb of Jerusalem that has been the subject of a decadeslong property dispute between private parties and in which Arabs who aren't subject to such disputes continue to live.

The conflict between Hamas and Israel is about a stubborn fact: Israel exists, and Hamas wishes it didn't exist. Hamas will target civilians in Israel, use Palestinian children to shield its rockets and lie to the press to achieve its goals. Israel, meanwhile, is seeking to minimize civilian casualties at great risk to its own citizens.

Opposing Israel's actions doesn't make you an anti-Semite. But siding with Hamas in a conflict like this one certainly does.

China Isn't Winning. The West Is Forfeiting

May 26, 2021

This week, The Wall Street Journal reported that three researchers from the Chinese Wuhan Institute of Virology were hospitalized in November 2019 with "symptoms consistent with both Covid-19 and common seasonal illness." That report followed hard on a series of investigative pieces from journalists such as Nicholas Wade and Donald McNeil, formerly of The New York Times, who revived the media-dismissed theory that the institute had generated COVID-19 in a laboratory and then accidentally allowed it to leak. "The argument that it *could* have leaked out of the Wuhan Institute of Virology or a sister lab in Wuhan has become considerably stronger," McNeil wrote. "And China's lack of candor is disturbing."

It now seems highly credible that COVID-19 originated inside a Chinese state laboratory—and that China knew about it as early as November. In mid-January, the World Health Organization reported, based on Chinese information, that "Preliminary investigations conducted by the Chinese authorities have found no clear evidence of human-to-human transmission of the novel #coronavirus." China censured its own Dr. Li Wenliang for attempting to spread the news of COVID-19's danger. It took until the end of January for China to lock down Wuhan.

We'll never know the answers to those questions, because the same WHO that covered for China in the early days of the pandemic is responsible for investigating Chinese malfeasance today. And President Biden's administration seems happy to keep it that way. Asked about whether America would lead an independent investigation into COVID-19's Chinese origins, White House press secretary Jen Psaki stated, "We have repeatedly called for the WHO to support an expert-driven evaluation of the pandemic's origins that is free from interference and politicization."

Meanwhile, this week, actor John Cena apologized to the Chinese government. Cena, who stars in the upcoming "F9," was being interviewed by a Taiwanese television station and committed the grave offense of stating that "Taiwan is the first country that can watch" the movie. China, of course, sees Taiwan as an outlying territory of China and denies Taiwanese sovereignty. So, Cena, whose film has already grossed over $100 million in China, quickly issued an apology in Mandarin, saying: "I made a mistake. Now I have to say one thing which is very, very, very important: I love and respect China and the Chinese people."

The common thread here is a Western unwillingness to face down China's authoritarian regime. For some on the left, challenging China means standing up for Western values like democracy and human rights—and this, in turn, raises questions about America's own commitment to those principles. For some in corporate America, capitalism hasn't opened China but made the West more dependent on mercantilist Beijing.

"We're in competition with China and other countries to win the 21st century," Biden said in his recent quasi-State of the Union address. "We're at a great inflection point in history." China's possible unwitting release of COVID-19 and its fully documented cover-up is a unique opportunity to recalibrate the West's relationship with China. But there seems to be little taste for that necessary recalibration from a wavering Europe and United

States.

Meanwhile, China isn't wavering. China grows increasingly aggressive: through its Belt-and-Road Initiative, its militaristic advances in the South China Sea and its international ties with European countries happy to make concessions. China doesn't have to defeat the United States. All it has to do is outlast us. And right now, thanks to an ugly combination of hesitancy, cowardice and corruption, China seems well-positioned to do so.

What Foreign Dissidents Understand About the American Flag

July 14, 2021

This week, thousands of Cuban dissidents marched against the repressive communist tyranny that has subjugated the Cuban people for three generations. They chanted "Libertad!" and called for the end of the regime. And they carried aloft a symbol of freedom: the American flag.

This isn't a rarity. It's a common sight among protesters for freedom worldwide. Before Hong Kong was turned into yet another municipality of the Chinese communist tyranny, freedom-seeking dissidents marched by the tens of thousands, carrying the American flag. When Iranian protesters stand up against the mullahcracy subjecting their nation to theocratic despotism, they refuse to deface the American flag.

They do so for a reason: people all over the world understand that the American flag stands for freedom. The people of Britain and France understood it in 1917 just as they did in 1944. The prisoners of Auschwitz understood it; the freedom fighters in Hungary and Poland and Czechoslovakia understood it; South Korean patriots understood it; the Kurds understood it. For generations, the Stars and Stripes has been a symbol of liberty to all those across the planet who dissent from totalitarianism.

Which is why it is so striking that while foreign dissidents risk their very lives for their liberty to carry the American flag, American citizens who live in the freest, most prosperous, most racially tolerant nation in world history kneel for the flag, or burn the flag, or turn their backs on the flag. What do those abroad know that those at home don't? That totalitarianism is far more common throughout the world, and throughout world history, than freedom; that individual rights may be universal, but they only manifest when those with the courage of their convictions fight for them; that in a world of darkness and chaos, America—for all of its flaws, both historic and present—has been and remains a force for good.

And yet today's domestic Left can't say that much. When White House press secretary Jen Psaki was asked about the obvious disparity between Cuban dissident treatment of the American flag and American Leftist treatment of that same flag, she stammered, "Well, I would say first, the president certainly values and respects the symbol of the American flag. He's someone who certainly waves it outside of his house, or does in Delaware and other places where he's lived throughout his time. He also believes that people have the right to peaceful protests, and he thinks both can be true."

But that's not the question. The question is whether it is morally *right* to scorn the flag, not whether Americans have the right to do stupid things. The fact that the White House cannot simply acknowledge that foreign dissidents have it right about the American flag, and that many on today's American Left have it dead wrong, is telling and tragic.

It's tragic because a country that doesn't believe enough in its own principles to defend its flag on moral grounds—especially the flag representing a country that has freed hundreds of millions of people from tyranny and poverty—will cease to project its core principles. And freedom fighters abroad will pay the price. The American flag will stop being a symbol of freedom and hope, and instead become just what its critics now say it is: a symbol of weakness and solipsism.

If Americans believe that our flag is less a beacon of hope than a looming specter of oppression, we will withdraw from the world stage as we tend to the business of undermining and extirpating our foundational ideals. Which, of course, is the goal of the American Left. And the global power vacuum won't be filled by liberal elites, but by totalitarian powers who aren't nearly as apologetic about their own ambitions.

The Demise of the Love Gov

August 11, 2021

This week, Gov. Andrew Cuomo of New York resigned his office. It was a stunning turnabout for a man who had been proclaimed a hero of the republic by the entire media just last year, even as he presided over the worst COVID-19 spike in the United States and covered up the deaths of thousands of nursing-home patients. Trevor Noah declared himself a "Cuomosexual"; Chelsea Handler gushed about her "crush"; there was even talk about supplanting President Joe Biden with Cuomo at the top of the 2020 Democratic ticket were Biden to falter. Crown Publishing saw fit to shower $5 million in advance money on Cuomo's self-flattering COVID-19 memoir, humbly titled "American Crisis: Leadership Lessons from the COVID-19 Pandemic."

Now, of course, Cuomo isn't being dumped by the side of the road because of his horrific performance with regard to COVID-19, despite the fact that his state currently carries the second worst deaths-per-million ratio in the United States (Florida, the media's favorite bugaboo, ranks 26th by this metric, despite its status as America's oldest state outside of Maine). Far from it. Upon Cuomo's resignation, Biden lamented that Cuomo had done a "hell of a job" on "everything from access to voting infrastructure to a whole range of things. That's why it's so sad."

Instead, Cuomo was forced into resignation because of his habit of touching subordinates' body parts. Attorney General Letitia James, who has her own eyes on the gubernatorial mansion, put out a 168-page report detailing Cuomo's treatment of 11 different women who alleged sexual harassment; the most egregious allegation came from Brittany Commisso, a former aide, who said that Cuomo had rubbed her butt, kissed her on the lips and grabbed her breast under her shirt. James declined to prosecute Cuomo or recommend his prosecution, but her report was enough to open the floodgates. By the end of last week, it was clear that Cuomo didn't have any support in the halls of power to remain as governor—at least partially due to his long-standing habit of treating legislators like trash.

Now we're told that Cuomo's ousting is the result of Democrats' high moral standards. Joy Reid of MSNBC bragged that Cuomo's departure was "100% the result of Democratic pressure"—true as far as it goes, given Democrats currently comprise a supermajority in the New York state Senate. Russell Berman of The Atlantic made the same argument, stating, "Democrats hold their leaders to higher standards than Republicans do."

Of course, that isn't true. At all. Democrats routinely overlook powerful politicians accused of sexual misconduct, from the late Sen. Edward "Ted" Kennedy to former President Bill Clinton to Biden himself. It all depends on the politics of the moment. And the reality is that Cuomo was a liability for Democrats not merely because of his penchant for grabbing asses, but because his COVID-19 performance *was* so abysmal. Cuomo's lockdown policies resulted in extraordinary numbers of deaths, residents fleeing the state and the fourth-worst unemployment rate in the nation—even as Democrats championed him as a model governor.

Getting rid of Cuomo, then, was good politics. It allows Democrats to pretend that they care deeply about the #MeToo movement while simultaneously ridding themselves of a rather nettlesome problem. That's why it must be so galling for Cuomo—who has gotten away with egregious interpersonal behavior for at least a decade—to have to resign in his supposed moment of triumph. It's also why Democrats *must* defenestrate him: To acknowledge that Cuomo botched COVID-19 would be to acknowledge that Democrats' current policies mirror Cuomo's botchery. Better to brush Cuomo under the rug than for Cuomo's opponents to continue holding him up as an object lesson in dictatorial and bloviating incompetence.

America's Slow Suicide

September 1, 2021

Greek mythology tells the tale of Erysichthon, the powerful King of Thessaly. The story goes that Erysichthon, seeking wood, ordered the trees in a sacred grove to be cut. When his workers refused, fearing divine retribution, he did it himself; for this he was cursed. The curse placed upon Erysichthon was simple: unending hunger. In the end, Erysichthon ended up selling his daughter into slavery for the money to buy more food. Eventually, Erysichthon, lacking the resources to feed himself, ate his own body.

A nation that understands itself—that understands its purpose in the world—flourishes. Such nations, historically, have not shied away from their part on the stage of history. They have recognized a simple truth: In the game of power, vacuums are filled, generally by those who are most aggressive. And thus, surrender of the good means victory for the bad.

Historically, America has understood this. America has always been uncomfortable with the realities of foreign policy but has never shied away from its actual role as a player on the world stage. Yes, America was geographically removed from Europe, but that didn't stop America from competing with the French, British and Spanish empires. It was Thomas Jefferson, writing to his presidential successor James Madison, who said in 1809, "we should have such an empire for liberty as she has never surveyed since the creation: & I am persuaded no constitution was ever before so well calculated as ours for extensive empire & self-government." It was James Monroe in 1823 who declared that "the American continents, by the free and independent condition which they have assumed and maintain, are henceforth not to be considered as subjects for future colonization by any European powers."

A powerful America was good, and a powerful America was necessary.

When nations lose themselves—when nations destroy their sacred groves—they open a hole in themselves. That hole is ever-growing, ever-gnawing. And it cannot be satiated.

But that's just it: the hunger is itself the satisfaction. Our hunger gives us a mission. We must cure all inequality, even inequality caused by differences in behavior—the unavoidable condition of humanity—by spending trillions of dollars not yet created. We must rectify the imbalances of history—the unavoidable condition of humanity—by skewing all institutions toward "equity." We must abandon our prior foreign policy commitments—and our real foreign policy interests—in the name of quixotic attempts to "build back better" at home. We must rewrite the basic social compact in order to alleviate all natural differences between human beings.

We must sacrifice our sons and daughters to our hunger. We must teach them idiotic doctrines about complete human malleability, training them for confusion and chaos. We must indoctrinate them with the evils of our own philosophy, while teaching them that cultural diversity mandates that we overlook the far greater evils of other cultures. We must demand that our children protect us, rather than protecting our children. And, of course, we must snarl them in a web of debt not of their own making, condemning them to a future footing our bills.

And then, in the end, we eat ourselves. We turn on each other, recognizing that our mission has been lost and that our hunger can't satisfy us. We treat each other as enemies while downplaying the actual presence of actual enemies.

And then we disappear.

Or, alternatively, we don't.

We realize that whatever our faults, whatever our shortcomings, we have a role in the world; that whatever our faults, whatever our shortcomings, we still are heirs to the greatest founding philosophy in world history; that whatever our faults, whatever our shortcomings, we are still citizens of the same body politic.

The choice is still in our hands.

But if Afghanistan is any indicator, it's quickly slipping away.

Our Elective Monarchy

September 15, 2021

In 1629, frustrated by the unwillingness of Parliament to grant him taxation power, King Charles I of England dissolved the body and had nine members arrested. He did not recall Parliament for over a decade. The intervening period, known as Personal Rule, saw Charles I govern as a de facto dictator, with only a body of councilors to advise him. In 1640, forced by military necessity from Scotland, Charles I recalled Parliament in order to raise money to pay the military; shortly thereafter, stymied by Parliament, he dissolved the body again. But necessity encroached once again, and Charles I finally recalled Parliament. This would be the beginning of the end of his monarchy: the Long Parliament, as it would later be called, directly opposed many of Charles I's initiatives, and that opposition would devolve into the English Civil War—a war that ended with Charles I's execution.

All of this should serve as a brief reminder that when a chief executive ignores checks and balances, he may maximize his authority temporarily. But after a while, the royal saddle tends to chafe.

We are now approaching an inflection point in the United States: Do we want an elective monarchy, or not? A great many Americans seem perfectly comfortable with such a system, so long as the president is of their party. Today, the president of the United States is elected once every four years; he mouths platitudes about respect for norms and institutions; and then he proceeds to do what he wants, using the authority of the administrative state as his scepter. The legislature has become a vestigial organ, delegated only the power to fund enormous omnibus packages. True rule-making authority lies with the chief executive.

Thus, former President Barack Obama declared more than 20 times that he did not have the authority to unilaterally suspend elements of immigration law. That did not stop him from doing just that with the Deferred Action for Childhood Arrivals program. President Joe Biden recently declared he had no power to extend an eviction moratorium via the Centers for Disease Control and Prevention. That did not stop him from pursuing precisely that policy. Biden and his administration stated repeatedly that they did not have the power to unilaterally mandate COVID-19 vaccination. That power was to be exercised by the individual states. That did not stop Biden from mobilizing the vague grant of power under the Occupational Safety and Health Act to dictate that every business with more than 100 employees had to test its unvaccinated employees once per week, or vaccinate them, or fire them, or pay $14,000 per violation.

There are only two institutions standing in the way of full-fledged presidential monarchy: the courts and the states. Biden has pledged to override the states: "If these governors won't help us beat the pandemic, I'll use my power as president to get them out of the way." And while Biden has pledged not to stack the courts, his prior institutional pledges have lasted only as long as his power remains unchallenged; he repeatedly suggested he would not seek to destroy the filibuster but has now apparently flipped on that subject.

The problem with elective monarchy is that it destroys the feedback mechanisms that help balance a pluralistic, decentralized society. Charles I could reign under the precepts of Personal Rule just so long as his impositions were moderate and his foreign policy peaceful.

The minute serious complications arose, Personal Rule began to collapse.

The same will hold true in the United States. Charles I had the authority of kingship, but not consolidated compulsory control. That made his dictatorship unstable. The lesson for us is simple: We may want change, and we may want to carve a path through the checks and balances that obstruct that change by granting near-total power to an elective monarch. But unity won't follow. Chaos will.

The Red Wave, and the Democratic Suicide Strategy

November 3, 2021

This week, reality struck back against Democratic electoral utopianism. Since 2012, Democrats have been convinced that a new, durable, near-unbeatable political coalition was in the making: a coalition largely comprised of college-educated white voters, women, younger Americans and racial minorities. This coalition would overtake the demographically shrinking "old, white majority" and win victory after victory. As Ruy Teixeira and John Halpin wrote for the Center for American Progress in the aftermath of Obama's reelection, "Obama's strong progressive majority—built on a multi-racial, multi-ethnic, cross-class coalition in support of an activist... is real and growing and it reflects the face and beliefs of the United States in the early part of the 21st Century." CAP called this new strategy "the culmination of a decades-long project to build an electorally viable and ideologically coherent progressive coalition in national politics."

Ever since 2012, Democrats have been chasing that chimera. Instead of seeing Obama's 2012 victory as a testament to Obama's unique political skill, they have doubled down on the CAP strategy: more progressivism, more race-based politics. When that strategy failed in 2016, they chalked it up to Russian election interference and Facebook propaganda. When President Joe Biden won election in 2020, they announced that their strategy had been vindicated—even though the election was rather obviously a referendum on former President Donald Trump personally, not proof of their strategic brilliance.

And so, Democrats misread the tea leaves. Biden was elected to do two things: be Not Trump and restore a sense of moderation and stability to the White House. He has succeeded in the first, mainly because nobody is Trump. He has utterly failed in the second. That's because Biden rejected the central premise of his own candidacy, calling for more social spending than any president in history, abandoning Afghanistan to the Taliban for no apparent geostrategic reason, embracing the radical language of anti-racist activists, cramming down the restrictive COVID-19 policies via the administrative state and characterizing his opponents as bigots and Jan. 6-adjacent domestic terrorists. Biden Mini-Me's like Terry McAuliffe in Virginia have imitated the strategy.

The result, predictably, was disaster—not just in Virginia, but across the country. In Virginia, a state Biden won by 10 points, McAuliffe went down in flames, a black female Republican became lieutenant governor, a Cuban American became attorney general, and the GOP took the House of Delegates; in New Jersey, a no-name candidate ran dead even with media-feted Democratic Gov. Phil Murphy; in Buffalo, New York, Sen. Chuck Schumer-endorsed democratic socialist India Walton imploded against a write-in candidate; in Minneapolis, the "defund the police" movement shattered on the rocks of reality, with voters overwhelmingly rejecting the dismantling of the police department; in New York City, Eric Adams became mayor and quickly pledged to work with new Republican city council members.

Now, Democrats have a choice. They can either tack back to the center—stop pushing a "Build Back Better" grab bag of spending that is unpopular and unnecessary—or they can push forward. They can stop pressing the language of the 1619 Project in public school education—or they can demand that parents shut up. They can double down on progressivism or try to find a Clintonian third way.

Right now, it looks like they'll embrace more cowbell. The media and Democratic response to Virginia seems to be more spending; more labeling parental opposition to radicalism as racist and homophobic; more jabbering about Trump and Jan. 6 to distract from their own failures.

It's a bold strategy, Cotton. We'll see how it works out for them.

But for Democrats, a serious appraisal of the political landscape—an appraisal that might end with the realistic assessment that Obama's coalition is not inevitable, that there are swing voters in America, that policy ought to be directed toward every voter—might just be too difficult. Better to live in a fantasy world in which Obama is president forever, his coalition is durable and stable, and more progressivism is always the answer.

But 2022 is coming. And fantasy will meet reality once again for a Democratic Party committed to fundamental untruths about the American public.

Putin Wakes up the Western Ostrich

March 2, 2022

After the end of the Cold War, foreign policy experts across the spectrum assured us that things had changed. Wars of pure border conquest were over. Wars over oil would soon be a thing of the past. Instead, the increasingly intertwined world would move toward peace. Thomas Friedman suggested in his massive 1999 bestseller "The Lexus and the Olive Tree" that no two countries with McDonald's would go to war with each other; Francis Fukuyama stated in "The End of History and the Last Man" that we had reached the "end-point of mankind's ideological evolution and the universalization of Western liberal democracy as the final form of human government."

The West set about proving these dubious theses by embracing what could be termed an ostrich foreign policy: a willingness to place security considerations last, and to pursue utopian goals with alacrity. Germany spent decades making itself more dependent on Russian natural gas and oil in order to pursue the dream of green energy, meanwhile slashing its defense budget as a percentage of GDP. France acted similarly. So did the United Kingdom.

The West banked instead on more economic interdependence via the International Monetary Fund and World Trade Organization, more diplomacy at Davos and the United Nations.

Most of all, the West banked on its own unwillingness to recognize reality. When, in 2012, Mitt Romney made the crucial error of reminding Americans that Russia was a geopolitical foe, President Barack Obama openly mocked him. So did Obama's complaint media. The 1980s had called, and they wanted their foreign policy back.

When aggressive global competitors made clear that they did not buy into the West's vision of a grand and glorious materialist future combined with welfare statism—that they believed their own national histories had yet to be fully written, and that their centuries-old territorial ambitions were still quite alive—the West simply looked the other way. When Russia invaded Georgia in 2008, the West did nothing. When Russia invaded Crimea in 2014, the West did nothing. When China abrogated its treaty with the U.K. and took over Hong Kong in 2020, the West did nothing. And, of course, President Joe Biden precipitously removed American support for the Afghan regime, toppling it in favor of the Taliban.

The West decided that it would make a war-free future a reality by simply ending war.

Now, as the West is finding out, ending war is a game that requires two players. Russian President Vladimir Putin saw Western weakness as the impetus for his final grand strategic move: the destruction and occupation of Ukraine. And the West has been shocked back into reality: yes, opponents of American hegemony are territorially ambitious; yes, they want more than mere integration into world markets; yes, they are willing to murder and invade in order to achieve their goals. Times and technologies may change, but human nature remains the same.

As George Orwell wrote in 1940 about the rise of the Nazis, "Nearly all western thought since the last war, certainly all 'progressive' thought, has assumed tacitly that human beings desire nothing beyond ease, security and avoidance of pain... Hitler, because in his own joyless mind he feels it with exceptional strength, knows that human beings don't only want comfort, safety, short working-hours, hygiene, birth-control and, in general, common sense; they also, at least intermittently, want struggle and self-sacrifice, not to mention drums, flags and loyalty-parades."

The West rose to meet Hitler's challenge. It appears that the West is rising again to meet the challenge of Russian aggression. We can only hope that the West's newfound commitment to a very old idea—the idea that only a sense of Western purpose combined with some very hardheaded thinking about hard power can preserve freedom—lasts longer than Putin's invasion. If it doesn't, the reshaping of the world order will continue, to the lasting detriment of a West that is only now removing its head from the sand.

Environmentalist NIMBYism Means Foreign Policy Disaster

March 9, 2022

    This week, as the Russian invasion of Ukraine dragged on, gas prices in America soared to their highest levels since 2008, increasing over 57 cents in just one month. In parts of the United States, gas at the pump costs in excess of $7 per gallon.

    The answer to this challenge is obvious: The United States ought to open the drilling floodgates. In 2019, net imports of crude oil and finished products were exceeded by American exports of such products for the first time on record. That was due to the massive increase in American production thanks to fracking over the course of the prior decade. This did not mean that the United States had stopped importing crude oil. But as of 2019, we were importing some 3.8 million barrels of crude oil per day, radically down from over 10 million in 2005. More production, generally speaking, means less dependence.

    And that matters, as we're now seeing. Europe, which is far more dependent on foreign oil than the United States, has seen its energy prices skyrocket since the Russian invasion. That's why Germany's Chancellor Olaf Scholz announced, "Europe has deliberately exempted energy supplies from Russia from sanctions. Supplying Europe with energy for heat generation, mobility, electricity supply and industry cannot be secured in any other way at the moment." U.K. Prime Minister Boris Johnson agreed: "I think there are different dependencies in different countries, and we have to be mindful of that."

    So now would be an excellent time for the United

States to grab muscular leadership of the world energy markets. Instead, the Biden administration—which opted upon taking office to undercut the oil and gas industry and radically subsidize inefficient "green energy" production—has decided to seek energy aid from some of the world's worst dictatorships. This week, the Biden administration sent emissaries to the Venezuelan dictator Nicolas Maduro in an attempt to increase oil imports from the socialist hellhole. White House press secretary Jen Psaki said, "The purpose of the trip that was taken by administration officials was to discuss a range of issues, including certainly energy security."

Meanwhile, Juan Guaido, leader of the Venezuelan opposition, was left out in the cold. "It is foolish to think that Maduro will quit Russia," he quite logically explained. "This is a mistake. To buy oil from Maduro is the same as buying oil from Putin."

But this is the point: For the international Left, dependency on oil-driven authoritarian states is *preferable* to energy independence. It allows Left-wing leaders the privilege of appeasing their environmentalist base while at the same time keeping energy prices low. Carbon-based emissions are too hideous to be considered so long as they're being produced on American or European soil—but we're perfectly willing to subsidize Russian President Vladimir Putin, Maduro and the Iranian ayatollahs to exploit the environment and enrich themselves while promoting tyranny at home and abroad, so long as Greta Thunberg isn't disappointed in us.

And so we continue to promote the abject idiocy of Secretary of Transportation Pete Buttigieg, who recommended to those suffering from high gas prices that they just shell out for an electric vehicle. We continue to nod along to the stupidity of Psaki, who agreed that the solution to $7-a-gallon gas was "getting the whole country off of fossil fuels." Then we import our energy from the world's worst despots.

Opposition to oil and gas development has always been the privilege of rich countries; we simply outsourced the pollution and environmental degradation elsewhere. But as it turns out, in the end, we all pay the price for our willingness to pay off autocrats just so we can temporarily pretend that we did our bit for Greenpeace.

Push Where There's Mush

March 16, 2022

There is no substitute for American strength. When America's enemies find weakness, they exert pressure. And today, America's enemies are finding weakness at nearly every turn.

Vladimir Lenin supposedly stated that his preferred foreign policy strategy was to "probe with bayonets: if you find mush, you push. If you find steel, you withdraw." Vladimir Putin follows the same strategy. This week, as his forces shell Kyiv and batter Kharkiv, Putin has been upping the ante. He has unleashed strikes against Ukrainian targets near the Polish border, tacitly threatening to attack a NATO member. He continues to leverage his natural gas and oil supply to hold Europe hostage. His foreign policy apparatus continues to threaten the possibility of wider war should the West send in further armaments including MiGs sufficient to repel the Russian invasion. He has reached out to China for support. And he has utilized America's overweening desire for some sort of Iranian nuclear deal to press for American concessions on evading sanctions.

All of Putin's pressure has met with mixed response. The West has continued shipments of certain types of materiel, including Javelin and Stinger missiles. But this week, the Biden administration signaled first that it would allow shipment of MiGs to Ukraine, then backed off, claiming that such shipments might amount to escalation. Meanwhile, the West's economic sanctions are being maintained—but Russia announced this week that the United States had made written concessions that would exempt Russia's ability to trade with Iran, despite Iran firing missiles at a U.S. consulate in Erbil, Iraq.

What's the chief message from all of this waffling? That the West's threats are, at best, sporadically credible. Russia believes that if it ramps up the pressure harshly enough on Ukraine and threatens the West enough with nuclear war, it will be able to pry out of Ukraine diplomatically what it has been unable to pry out of Ukraine militarily—and Russia may well succeed. After all, Germans can't continue to pay $8.25 per gallon for gas forever.

At the same time, China, which has been playing both sides against the middle, is watching. China has been offering itself out as a "neutral mediator" between Russia and the West, despite the fact that China is an out-and-out Putin ally. China has been buying up troubled Russian assets at bargain-basement prices, strengthening both their connections with Russia and their portfolio—and meanwhile, China has received little credible threat of blowback from the West, which does not want to exacerbate inflationary problems by intensifying supply chain issues. As The New York Times reported, "a consensus is forming in Chinese policy circles that one country stands to emerge victorious from the turmoil: China." Investors are beginning to worry about the possibility of a Chinese invasion of Taiwan.

Nonaligned countries are increasingly skittish about Western promises. It is no coincidence that as Team Biden reaches out to Iran via Russia, Saudi Arabia has declined to take Biden's phone calls and instead reached out to China. It is no wonder that India, which buys exorbitant amounts of weaponry from Russia to counter China and Pakistan, has refused to denounce Russia. When the West wavers, it becomes a bad bet.

Western deterrence already failed in Ukraine. If the West fails to reestablish deterrence in the next phase of global geopolitics, the results will be even more dire, and the realignment currently playing out will only accelerate—to the detriment of the U.S. and her allies.

The Death of The Elite "Center"

June 22, 2022

The false center cannot hold.

In France, President Emmanuel Macron has now lost his majority in the National Assembly; his party holds 245 seats in the lower house, but the Right holds 150 and the Left 131. In Colombia, former M-19 guerrilla and Marxist Gustavo Petro has now become the president of the country, replacing more establishment, Keynesian liberal rule. In the United States, the supposed center within both parties has been increasingly supplanted by anti-establishment forces on both sides.

None of this should be shocking, given the destruction of institutional trust throughout the West. And the destruction of that institutional trust has been well earned: It represents the natural result of policy elites lying to those they supposedly serve. Our policy elites maintain that they favor free markets while simultaneously battling against free markets on behalf of a world-changing ideology; they proclaim that they value traditional religion while fighting to undermine its most fundamental foundations; they argue that the world order must be maintained while shying away from the reality of international politics.

Klaus Schwab, the head of the World Economic Forum, supposedly a repository of free market thinking, declares that he and his friends will "serve not only self-interest, but we serve the community"; he then proceeds to leverage economic power on behalf of their preferred ideological outcomes. The result is both economic failure and ideological failure. Take, for example, the Biden administration's simultaneous demand that oil companies ramp up production and that we completely undermine oil and gas development over the next few years in order to fight global warming. Or, more immediately, take the German attempts to "green" their own economy while quietly outsourcing energy production to Russia—a policy so egregiously stupid that it has now resulted in Germany firing up coal plants again, now that Russia has cut off the oil supply.

On the social front, our institutional elite declare fealty to traditional institutions—church, family, localism—and then simultaneously insist that society remake itself in the most radical possible image. House Speaker Nancy Pelosi declares her fealty to Catholicism in the same sentence in which she militantly maintains her support for abortion-on-demand; President Joe Biden proclaims his own religiosity while simultaneously deploying his Department of Justice to target states that seek to prevent the confusion and mutilation of children based on nonsensical gender theory.

On the foreign policy front, our institutional leaders tell us that we must uphold the world order, then refuse to accept the consequences of that leadership. They rail against the evils of the Saudi Arabian regime while simultaneously intoning that the West must sign a deal with the Iranian terror regime, then end up visiting the Saudis to beg for more oil production. They declare their undying support for the Ukrainian government, then become wishy-washy about providing either the support necessary for its victory or an exit plan in case victory is unachievable. They look askance at the Chinese threat to Taiwan, then teach proper transgender pronoun use to members of the Navy.

In short, our institutional elites rely on the power of civilizational foundations that long predate them—free markets, religious values, military strength—to prop up failing ideas that undermine those foundations. The result is failure. The Left looks at the prevailing elite consensus and declares it dishonest: If the elites' principles mattered, they would fight free markets, religious values and military strength. The Right looks at the prevailing elite consensus and feels the same way: If the elites put aside their ideological commitments to leftism, they'd cement our civilizational foundations rather than keep eroding them.

Perhaps the center isn't holding because it *shouldn't* hold. That center has sought to enshrine its own power by taking from both the Left and the Right; it has no coherent ideology of its own. And that false center is now coming apart with centrifugal force, torn between those who believe in the fundamental institutions of the West and those who wish to see them supplanted.

The Chinese Know We're in Cold War II. It's Time for Us to Understand the Same.

July 27, 2022

This week, the Chinese government announced its fierce opposition to Speaker of the House Nancy Pelosi, D-Calif., visiting Taiwan. Chinese Foreign Ministry spokesperson Zhao Lijian said that China was "fully prepared… If the U.S. is bent on going its own way, China will take firm and strong measures to defend national sovereignty and territorial integrity." In response, the Biden administration announced its discomfort with Pelosi's visit: Biden told journalists that military officials thought the trip was "not a good idea."

Meanwhile, The Wall Street Journal reported that the Chinese government had accelerated its push to reshore the manufacture of semiconductors. According to the Journal, "China is leading the world in building new chip factories, a step toward achieving more self-sufficiency in semiconductors that could eventually make some buyers reliant on China for many of the basic chips now in short supply." That news ought to be disquieting for those who understand the flow of semiconductors, the single most important commodity on the planet, a component of nearly every major technology used today. Taiwan manufactures approximately 92% of advanced semiconductors; South Korea manufactures nearly all of the rest.

China's dependence on foreign semiconductors is one of the world's best hedges against Chinese attacks on Taiwan: should China attack Taiwan, Taiwan could destroy its semiconductors and infrastructure. But if China can ramp up its own domestic manufacture while everyone else is behind, China is in a solid position to blackmail the world economy in the same way Russia has using its energy supply.

And China isn't unaware of their growing advantage. Gen. Mark Milley, chairman of the Joint Chiefs of Staff, said the Chinese have become far more aggressive in recent years; international relations expert Shi Yinhong, who works at Beijing's Renmin University, told the Associated Press that China "will take unprecedented tough measures and the U.S. must make military preparations" if Pelosi should visit.

So, what ought the West to do?

First, the United States must stop acting as though China will change its tack any time soon. Xi Jinping has upped the ante over recent months in advance of his next party congress; he is likely to continue upping the ante as his economic and demographic model turns upside down. The long-term future for China is dismal: China's economy is a paper tiger rooted in debt, and China simply doesn't have the population growth necessary to support its massive spending. This means that China sees its window for action closing.

Second, the United States must realize it is already in a Cold War II with the Chinese government. This means ramping up our own domestic economic capacity— unleashing the economy through deregulation, energy production and tax reduction; refunding the military at the levels necessary to sustain a two-front war, and rebuilding the navy, which has shrunk to ship numbers lower than the United States had preceding World War II; diversifying supply chains for goods and services necessary to the United States, reshoring those supply chains away from China; and cutting off China's access to cutting-edge technologies.

    This also means that the United States must refocus its energy and ire externally rather than internally. Americans have expended an enormous amount of time, money and energy on attacking one another, on turning inward; the result has been a cancerous politics that results in the continuing dissolution of our social capital. During the Cold War, most Americans understood that the enemy wasn't at home, it was the communist tyranny threatening the U.S. and her allies; during Cold War II, Americans must learn the same lesson again.

Buzzword Foreign Policy Makes for Failure

August 3, 2022

    This week, House Speaker Nancy Pelosi went to Taiwan, determined to make a statement about American support for the democratic country under constant threat from its tyrannical Chinese neighbor. That trip prompted spasms of apoplexy from the Chinese government, which vowed serious consequences; China, in the end, engaged mainly in some military posturing.

    There is no question that Pelosi is correct about the need for the West to support Taiwan, nor is there any question that China is an aggressive dictatorship. But Pelosi's trip represents the latest in a long line of American foreign policy moves that seem like bluster rather than strength. It's one thing for John F. Kennedy to fly to Berlin in the midst of a Cold War blockade of the city to show solidarity with Germans in the face of Soviet aggression, declaring that the United States would indeed defend West Berlin in case of invasion. It's another for Pelosi to fly to Taiwan in provocative defiance of Chinese caterwauling without any firm deliverable: no statement of American intention to defend Taiwan in case of invasion (President Joe Biden actually stated that America *would* do so, before his State Department then walked it back); no major increase in military aid to the island; no increase to the projective power of the United States Navy, which will purchase nine ships this year while losing 24.

    Pelosi's visit, therefore, sounds a lot like the virtue signaling in which American politicians of both parties have engaged for decades. These politicians say they will protect democratic allies, then abandon them when the going gets tough; they explain that their foreign policy priorities range from free elections to gay rights, then hobnob with the world's worst dictators. They speak loudly and carry a wet noodle. Their addiction to high-flown rhetoric and vacillating commitment undercuts both their credibility and their capacity for moral suasion.

Biden represents a paradigmatic example of this sort of politician: in February 2002, for example, he stated that "history will judge us harshly if we allow the hope of a liberated Afghanistan to evaporate because we failed to stay the course"; by 2021, Biden was pulling the plug on Afghanistan, handing the country over to the tender mercies of the very same people who presided over the planning of Sept. 11. Biden spent all of 2020 describing Saudi Arabia as a pariah over its human rights violations; by 2022, he was fist-bumping Crown Prince Mohammed Bin Salman.

The answer to a foreign policy based on buzzwords is a foreign policy based on forwarding American interests, which over the long run will indeed forward America's values. Instead of suggesting that America will defend Ukraine because of Ukraine's commitment to democracy, for example—a commitment that is undermined internally by rabid corruption—our leaders should simply tell the truth: We ought to defend Ukraine from Russia because it is in our interest to counter Russian predations in Europe, which threaten the integrity of our allies in NATO and foster more aggression from our geopolitical opponents including China. At least such a clear position would prevent the misunderstandings that arise when Western nations bluster about defending democracy, then repeatedly do nothing to do so, as the West did during Russia's invasions of Georgia and Crimea.

Such a foreign policy would be nothing new; it would be perfectly in line with the famous words of John Quincy Adams, who stated that America "goes not abroad, in search of monsters to destroy. She is the well-wisher to the freedom and independence of all. She is the champion and vindicator only of her own." America ought to know her own interests. And America ought to protect her own interests. At least then our allies and our enemies will know where we stand, rather than speculating that our rhetoric is empty.

Salman Rushdie, Iran and Joe Biden

August 17, 2022

In October 2018, agents of the Saudi Arabian government murdered columnist and Muslim Brotherhood fellow traveler Jamal Khashoggi in gruesome fashion. The fallout in the American media was cataclysmic for the relationship between the United States and Saudi Arabia; two years after the murder, then-candidate Joe Biden issued a statement "mourning Khashoggi's death" and calling for reassessment of the American relationship with the Kingdom.

This week, a 24-year-old Muslim American with connections to Iran's Islamic Revolutionary Guard Corps attempted to murder famed author Salman Rushdie for writing "The Satanic Verses." In 1989, the Iranian government issued its death sentence on Rushdie, encouraging anyone within its purview to kill him; in the aftermath of Rushdie's stabbing—Rushdie ended up on a ventilator and will likely lose an eye—the Iranian government issued a statement blaming Rushdie "and his supporters... We believe that the insults made and the support he received was an insult against followers of all religions."

Just days before the attack on Rushdie, a member of the IRGC was charged by the Justice Department in a murder-for-hire attempt on former national security adviser John Bolton. The attempt was reportedly retaliation for the American drone strike on IRGC commander Qasem Soleimani in 2020; the suspect tried to pay an undercover federal agent $300,000 for the killing.

A few weeks before that, a suspect carrying a loaded AK-47 was arrested outside the home of an Iranian

American journalist, Masih Alinejad. According to Alinejad, the Iranian government has promoted a widespread campaign requesting her kidnapping; last year, news broke that four Iranians had been arrested while planning to do just that.

Meanwhile, Iranian state media is calling for more violence; an editorial from Kayhan newspaper, the editor of which is chosen by the Ayatollah Ali Khamenei, stated this week, "God has taken his revenge on Rushdie. The attack on him shows it is not a difficult job to take similar revenge on Trump and Pompeo and from now on they will feel more in danger for their lives."

The response to all of this has been deafening from the Biden administration. The White House released an extraordinarily tepid statement "reaffirm(ing) our commitment" to "Truth. Courage. Resilience." Biden said that he stood "in solidarity with Rushdie and all those who stand for freedom of expression." There was no talk of reevaluating America's relationship with Iran.

Indeed, the precise opposite has happened. The Biden administration is pursuing a nuclear deal that would loosen sanctions on the Iranian regime while giving them a clear pathway to development of a nuclear weapon. Instead of viewing the Iranian regime as an intransigent supporter of international terrorism from New York to Yemen to the Gaza Strip to Syria to Lebanon to Iraq, the Biden White House has decided that it must cut a deal at all costs. The New York Times reported this week, "For the first time in many months, European officials expressed increasing optimism on Tuesday that a revival of the 2015 Iran nuclear deal may actually be agreed upon by Iran and the United States."

Biden's shocking alacrity in seeking a signature from the Iranian regime—a regime with the blood of thousands on its hands, including Rushdie's—demonstrates the abjectly foolish pusillanimity of this administration. It also shows the world's most radical regimes that radicalism will be tolerated by a Democratic White House so long as those regimes promise a revised balance of power in line with longtime Democratic shibboleths. Biden wishes Iran to be at the center of a revised Middle Eastern power balance, in line with the idiotic thought of former President Barack Obama; he is therefore willing to kowtow to the mullahs while breaking with the Saudis. If you are the Taliban, the Biden administration will surrender; if you are Iran, the Biden administration will prostrate itself. This isn't just cowardice. It's delusional cowardice. And it's dangerous, not just to Rushdie, Bolton, Pompeo and Trump, but to anyone who opposes predations by America's enemies.

Unserious Leadership in A Serious Time

September 7, 2022

We live in a deeply serious time with deeply unserious leaders.

Historian Niall Ferguson has written that the "extreme violence of the twentieth century" was precipitated by three preconditions: "ethnic conflict, economic volatility, and empires in decline." It is difficult not to see such preconditions repeating themselves in this century. The West is currently tearing itself apart over concerns about birthrate, immigration and multiculturalism. Economic volatility is raging: After a decades-long reshifting of manufacturing away from the West and a reorientation toward finance and service, the hollowing out of the Western energy sector in pursuit of utopian environmentalism—all punctuated by the Great Recession, the COVID-19 mini-depression and now sky-high rates of inflation—the global economy sits on a razor's edge.

And then there is the problem of empires in decline.

We tend to think of our world as empire-free, a world of nation-states. But that's not really correct. The United States, however hesitant, is a de facto empire, even if not in the colonialist mold of the British Empire; the European Union would, in any other context, be considered a continental empire; Russia has always considered itself an imperial power, and Vladimir Putin's invasion of Ukraine represents merely the latest iteration of this claim; China has an empire of its own, not merely a nation-state—as author Ai Weiwei recently wrote, "the people who live in

China or come from it are a jumble of more than 50 ethnic and linguistic groups."

The Russian empire is far past decline; it is an economic backwater armed with antiquated military systems, in grave demographic trouble. But China is the area of highest risk today. The Chinese economy underwent tremendous economic growth over the course of the last two decades, but that growth now appears to be stalling out: state-run mercantilism is not self-sustaining, and as China scholar Michael Pettis recently wrote, "China's excessive reliance on surging debt in recent years has made the country's growth model unsustainable... (it is likely) that the country will face a very long, Japan-style period of low growth." China's demographics are entirely upside-down; its population is expected to reduce by nearly 50% by 2100. And President Xi Jinping is about to declare himself dictator for life.

In all of this, China strongly resembles Nazi Germany on the precipice of territorial aggression against its neighbors. Nazi Germany saw tremendous GDP growth, rooted largely in debt, state-sponsored mercantilism and military spending; Germany's fertility rate dropped from above 4 children per woman in 1910 to well below 2 by 1935. Nazi Germany's underpinnings were fragile; Hitler saw his window closing. Military aggression was therefore not unpredictable.

So, what would China's next logical step be? Its eyes are fixed on Taiwan. Given China's historic lust for Taiwan and Taiwan's domination of the all-important production of sophisticated semiconductors, a Chinese invasion of the island would be not at all unpredictable.

Which brings us back to the deeply unserious leadership of the West.

Faced with the prospect of ethnic tensions, economic

volatility and the internal instability of China, the West is opting for weakness. Economic growth is the prerequisite for military power; moral strength is the prerequisite for internal cohesion. The West has decided, over the course of years, to abandon its commitment to economic strength, instead fighting a losing war with the climate and promising endless giveaways from the unfunded welfare state; simultaneously, the West has fallen into the self-doubt of dying civilizations, pitting its citizens against each other, labeling them "semi-fascists" and "threats to democracy." We lie somewhere between the moral collapse of Rudyard Kipling's "Recessional" (1897) and Philip Larkin's "Homage to a Government" (1969). This doesn't mean that the West is on the verge of collapse; China is far more vulnerable than we are. But it does spell a future of chaos and difficulty—the kind of chaos and difficulty only strength, economic and military and moral, can successfully keep at bay.

Forgetting 9/11

September 14, 2022

On the 21st anniversary of Sept. 11, President Joe Biden repeated the same tired nostrums we have heard for the past several years on the anniversary of the worst terror attack in American history: "We will never forget, we will never give up. Our commitment to preventing another attack on the United States is without end."

That, of course, was rather ironic coming from the president who surrendered Afghanistan to the Taliban, the very people in charge of the country when al-Qaida launched its attacks on the World Trade Center and Pentagon. It was Biden who declared his own heroism as he ushered in the revitalization of al-Qaida itself in Afghanistan; as The Washington Post noted in August, "After the attacks of September 11, 2001, the U.S. goal was to deny al-Qaida a haven in Afghanistan. Now, it is back—and seemingly safe."

But none of this should be unexpected. Whatever lessons Americans learned on 9/11 have largely been forgotten one generation later.

On 9/11, we learned that the world is smaller than we think—that retreating from the world is not an option, and that if we do so, our enemies take advantage. One generation later, both parties encourage quasi-isolationist foreign policy reminiscent of the Clinton era, in which terrorism was treated as a law enforcement problem and the United States attempted to cut its presence abroad.

On 9/11, we learned that perceived weakness in any form—economic, military or ideological—invites aggression from our enemies. One generation later, we are deliberately destroying our own energy policy, focusing on expanded and fiscally irresponsible welfare statism, cutting our military capacity and pursuing radical ideological dissolution.

On 9/11, we learned that we have more in common than we do that separates us. One generation later, the president of the United States speaks about his fellow citizens as threats to democracy and declares that those who don't deal with him are existential problems for the republic.

In the aftermath of 9/11, we learned that cultural and political change in foreign countries takes time, investment and blood. One generation later, we continue to pretend that democratic values will inevitably spread around the globe—that there is a "right side of history" that will simply manifest itself—and that exporting cultural Leftism is a necessary component of our foreign policy.

Overall, we learned on 9/11 that the world is a chaotic and terrible place in which the right may not always triumph and the wrong may do the decent terrible damage. One generation later, we seem to have forgotten that simple lesson, instead regressing to a sort of puerile innocence in which we are constantly shocked by brutal realities. This is not a recipe for safety, prosperity or success.

German Chancellor Otto von Bismarck once remarked, "There is a Providence that protects idiots, drunkards, children and the United States of America." If America repeats the idiocies of its past, it will have to rely on that Providence once more to protect us—for surely our leaders will not.

The International Anti-Woke Backlash

September 28, 2022

This week, Italy prepared to welcome a new prime minister: 45-year-old Giorgia Meloni, leader of the right-wing Brothers of Italy party since 2014. Meloni is a populist conservative on issues ranging from marriage to immigration; she is a nationalist by philosophy and combatively passionate by temperament. A clip of a speech she gave at the World Congress of Families in 2019 has now gone viral with American conservatives; she explained, "Why is the family an enemy? Why is the family so frightening? There is a single answer to all these questions. Because it defines us. Because it is our identity. Because everything that defines us is now an enemy for those who would like us to no longer have an identity and to simply be perfect consumer slaves. And so they attack national identity, they attack religious identity, they attack gender identity, they attack family identity… We will defend God, country and family."

This speech, according to much of the media, represented an indicator of incipient fascism in the land of Benito Mussolini. Never mind that former Italian prime minister Matteo Renzi scoffed at such a notion, calling the "risk of fascism… absolutely fake news." The Intercept promptly called Meloni the "latest fascist womanhood icon." Ishaan Tharoor of The Washington Post railed that she's "set to be her country's most ultra-nationalist premier since fascist dictator Benito Mussolini."

Meloni is merely the latest recipient of such treatment internationally. In Sweden, the new government, supported by the right-wing Sweden Democrats, is already being touted as proto-fascist thanks to the origins of the SD. In Hungary, Prime Minister Viktor Orban has been treated as a knockoff of Vladimir Putin, despite the fact that he won his last election with a bare majority of 52.52% of the vote, increasing his vote share from 47.89% in 2018 and 44.87% in 2014. Polish Deputy Prime Minister Jaroslaw Kaczynski, leader of the Law and Justice Party, has been treated similarly; so have Brazilian President Jair Bolsonaro (currently trailing in the polls to socialistic former president Luiz Inacio Lula da Silva), and former and probable future Israeli Prime Minister Benjamin Netanyahu.

What, precisely, is the common thread linking these disparate politicians across a wide variety of countries? After all, none of these politicians are remotely like Vladimir Putin or Xi Jinping; none of them preside over authoritarian states. In fact, Left-wing politicians have engaged in far more intrusive antidemocratic measures over the past two years, from lockdowns to unilateral centralization of executive power.

The common thread is precisely the themes embraced by Meloni: national pride and rejection of Left-wing social values. The radical anti-traditionalism of the post-modernist Left, combined with the social apathy of centrists, has led to a serious international backlash. That backlash takes the form of a resurgent recognition that basic roles within societies must be protected, and that failure to do so is tantamount to national suicide.

And it is precisely that backlash that many in the media find so disquieting. To them, traditional roles are themselves fascist institutions; those who promote such roles suggest that human happiness can't be found in atomistic individualism, supplemented by collective social welfare schemes. And so true freedom requires that those like Meloni be fought.

Unfortunately for the Left, anti-traditionalism is the privilege of the frivolous—and after the failure of totalitarian COVID-19 policy, the collapse of green utopianism and the decay of societal solidarity, frivolity is no longer the order of the day. Which means that Meloni and those who agree with her are only the beginning.